AGS

YOU and the LAW

by
Ed Brandt

AGS®

American Guidance Service, Inc.
4201 Woodland Road
Circle Pines, MN 55014-1796
1-800-328-2560

Learning About Our United States

Cover photo credit: Images © 1996 Photo Disc, Inc.

Printed in the United States of America

ISBN 0–7854–0963–7 (Previously ISBN 0–88671–541–5)

Order Number: 90874

A 0 9 8 7 6 5 4

Contents

Foreword

Ignorance of the law excuse no man;
not that all men know the law,
but because 'tis an excuse every man will plead.
–John Selden

"I've got my rights!"

What does this statement mean? What are these rights you possess? Where do they come from? More importantly, what do these rights mean to your life? This book will help you understand not only your own rights, but what happens to you when you deny someone else his or her rights.

When you talk about your rights, you mean the rights guaranteed to you by the law. Your rights did not come out of thin air. They came from a body of law that has grown for more than 4,000 years. The people of the United States are guaranteed their rights by the United States Constitution.

Laws are not as complicated or confusing as they seem. They are based on common sense. Laws exist to protect one individual from another. They are also there to protect individuals from their government.

In this book we will explain what a crime is and what steps are taken after someone is arrested for committing a crime. You will learn what penalties a criminal might suffer, and what rights a person accused of a crime has. However, there is much more to the law than crime. The law also exists to settle disputes, or disagreements, among people.

History of the Law

The law is the witness and external deposit of our moral life.
Its history is the history of the moral development of the race.
—Oliver Wendell Holmes, Jr.

Words to Remember	
ancient	long ago The *ancient* Romans ruled much of Europe and the Middle East 2,000 years ago.
complicated	hard to follow or understand The puzzle was very *complicated*.
concept	something someone thought up; an idea It was Mr. Wright's *concept* that humans could fly.
vast	very big Russia is a *vast* country.

The **ancient** Romans are responsible for our present **concept** of law. The Romans ruled much of Europe and the Middle East about 2,000 years ago. At that time, the Romans knew about certain parts of the world including what is now Italy, Spain, France, Great Britain, the Middle East, parts of Germany, and even parts of Russia. The Romans did not know that North and South America existed.

The Romans believed in law and order. That was the only way they could rule such a **vast** empire. They took many of the best laws from other civilizations. These laws were combined into a new system that people could understand. Many laws today have stood the test of time because they have good reasons behind them.

English common law has also influenced the laws of today. This kind of law is based on the customs and habits of the people of England. It was called *common law* because the laws were commonly applied throughout the kingdom of ancient England. England was once a province (a division) of the Roman Empire, and the two systems of law mixed together. Parts of each are used in the United States today.

Laws are not as **complicated** and confusing as they seem. They are based on common sense. For example, if someone breaks a car window, he or she will be punished if caught. A fence cannot be built on someone else's property without permission. The law protects individuals and their belongings.

Imagine that there were no laws or police officers. Private property would not be respected. People could do as they pleased.

An ancient Roman named Gaius said that all laws should apply to persons, property, or procedure. Procedure means a method of dealing with something. This idea is still true today in the United States. The police have to follow a procedure when they arrest people. They have to tell them their rights and let them get a lawyer. If this procedure is not followed, the charges may be **nullified.** This procedure is a very important one to understand.

The most precious privileges of a Roman citizen were the guarding of person, property, and rights and **immunity** from torture or violence in the trying of a case. The law protected the **individual** from the state. This great privilege has been carried down to today in the United States. If any form of government hurts someone to make him or her confess to a crime, that government and its agents can be punished. This applies to any level of government, whether it be the city, state, or federal government.

There are other ideas that have been carried down to the present from Roman law. A Roman emperor named Antoninus said that if there is doubt about guilt or innocence, the case should be resolved in favor of the accused.

In the United States, the law says that a person accused must be found guilty beyond a "reasonable doubt" or this person must be set free.

The Romans believed that a person is **innocent** until proven guilty. This belief protects the citizen, especially when accused of committing a crime. For example, Linda was accused of breaking the window of an automobile. The state must gather all the evidence and then prove to a jury that Linda was the one who broke the window. In some countries, if someone is accused of a crime, the court believes that he or she is guilty until proven innocent.

	Words to Remember
immunity	protected; a condition of being able to resist harm or punishment. The person could not be punished for the crime because of his *immunity* from such proceedings.
individual	one person; a single thing or being That *individual* was seen crossing the street.
innocent	not guilty, doing no wrong In this country, an accused person is assumed to be *innocent* unless proven guilty.
nullify	wipe out; to make something worthless in the eyes of the law They decided to *nullify* their marriage.

Review Unit 1

A Write the letter of the best answer on the line.

_____ 1. Why do we have law?

    a. Law controls people.

    b. Law makes sense.

    c. Law protects individuals.

    d. Laws are complicated.

_____ 2. The ancient Romans ruled _____ of Europe and the Middle East.

    a. all

    b. most

    c. none

    d. about half

_____ 3. Laws are based on _____.

    a. history

    b. common sense

    c. Greek mythology

    d. procedures

_____ 4. In the United States, an accused person is _____.

    a. innocent until proven guilty

    b. guilty until proven innocent

    c. innocent without a doubt

    d. punished if caught

_____ 5. According to Gaius, law is connected to _____.

    a. persons

    b. property

    c. procedures

    d. all of the above

B Find each word in bold type in the text. Think about what the word means in that sentence. Then match the word to its definition by writing the correct letter on the line provided.

_____ 1. nullify   a. not guilty

_____ 2. innocent   b. an idea presented

_____ 3. individual   c. take away legal force

_____ 4. concept   d. from long ago

_____ 5. ancient   e. one

C Each of the following statements is *false*. Rewrite the statement correctly in the space provided.

1. The laws of the Romans are what we follow today.

_____

2. Romans believed that the only way to settle a dispute was to fight.

_____

3. Common law is based on the traditions and customs in France.

_____

4. In the United States, an accused person is automatically considered guilty.

_____

5. Laws protect the government from individuals.

_____

6. The law allows a police officer to push the suspect when making an arrest.

_____

7. American laws are based on what the President says.

_____

8. The Romans ruled much of North and South America 2,000 years ago.

_____

9. In the United States, government agents may use torture to force someone to confess to a crime.

_____

10. A method of dealing with something is called an *immunity*.

_____

11. An accused person can be found guilty even if there is reasonable doubt that he or she committed the crime.

_____

12. Gaius, an ancient Roman, said that if there is doubt about a person's guilt, the case should be found in favor of the accused.

_____

How Laws Help You

Besides helping resolve disputes, laws also tell people how to do things in order to prevent harm. Examples of these laws are

- driving laws
- property laws
- marriage and divorce laws
- food and drug safety laws
- laws licensing doctors, nurses, teachers, car drivers, etc.
- laws regulating car manufacturing
- laws regulating radio and television broadcasting

D Describe one situation in which you think each kind of law offers protection.

1. Driving laws:

_____

_____

2. Property laws:

_____

_____

3. Marriage or divorce laws:

_____

_____

4. Food and drug safety laws:

_____

_____

5. Licensing laws:

_____

_____

6. Regulation laws:

_____

_____

7. Broadcasting laws:

_____

_____

REVIEW

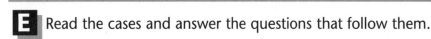 **E** Read the cases and answer the questions that follow them.

Case 1

The local convenience store was robbed twice in a month by the same person. The police investigated the crime by talking to witnesses, viewing the store's videotape, and gathering other evidence. They suspected that Avery Thompson committed the robberies. They arrested Thompson at his home. When they did, the police informed Thompson of his rights, including his right to have a lawyer present during questioning. They took Thompson to the police station and questioned him in the presence of his lawyer. Did the police follow procedures? Explain.

_____

_____

Case 2

Maura Goodwin was accused of stealing money from the office's petty cash drawer over a two-year period. At her trial, the prosecuting attorney proved that Goodwin had access to the petty cash, and she had worked there during the time the money was taken. The prosecution did not have any witnesses or information that showed only Goodwin could have taken the money. Goodwin's attorney proved that other people had access to the petty cash and that these people also worked in the office during the time that the money was taken. Should Goodwin be found guilty of stealing the money? Why or why not?

_____

_____

Case 3

The police forced three people out of their home and into a police car. The individuals were blindfolded and were given no information by the police. They were taken immediately to a prison where they were placed into a large cell. A year later, they were still in the prison. They were not told why they were in prison, and they were never brought to trial. They were not allowed to have visitors or any contact with anyone outside of the prison. Do you think this could happen in the United States? Why or why not?

_____

_____

The United States Constitution

We hold these truths to be self-evident, that all men are created equal, that they are endowed by their Creator with certain unalienable Rights, that among these are Life, Liberty and the Pursuit of Happiness.
—Thomas Jefferson, *The Declaration of Independence*

	Words to Remember
colony	a group of people who move to a new land, but still keep their ties to their former country People came from England many years ago and set up a *colony* in what is now the state of Maryland.
constitution	a set of rules by which people choose to be governed All American freedoms are guaranteed by the United States *Constitution.*
democracy	a form of government in which all the people share the power to govern In a *democracy*, the people run the government.
develop	to promote the growth of something by steps He exercised to *develop* his muscles. Some early Americans worked for many days to *develop* the Constitution.
goal	an end toward which you work It was his *goal* to become the strongest person in the world.
republic	a democracy in which people elect officials to run the government In a *republic,* the voters elect a president and congresspeople to make laws and run the country according to the wishes of its people.

When the thirteen American **colonies** declared their independence from Great Britain in 1776, they had to **develop** a new system of government. The colonies had been ruled by Great Britain, but now they were their own ruler. The intent of the American leaders was to make the most democratic **constitution** in the world. The leaders wanted a document that would guarantee freedom for all citizens and that would last a long time.

A **democracy** is a form of government in which people have the power to govern. One type of democracy is a **republic** in which the people run the government through elected representatives. A mayor, a congressional representative, and the President of the United State are all elected officials. They make decisions based on what the majority (more than half) of the people want. The United States is a democracy. It is also a republic.

One of the most important **goals** of the writers of the Constitution was to provide for the protection of the individual from the government. But first, the fifty-five delegates to the Constitutional Convention worked to set up the way their government would run. The writers of the Constitution divided the powers of the government into three branches. This separation of powers prevented one

branch of government from overpowering another. A system of checks and balances was also **implemented.** Each branch would operate independently but would check on the actions of the others. This prevents any person or group of people from running the country the way they want.

The delegates decided on seven "articles" of the Constitution. The first article **established** a legislative (lawmaking) body, which is called the *Congress.* The Congress is made up of two houses, or parts—the House of Representatives and the Senate. This arrangement is part of the system of checks and balances.

Words to Remember	
branch	a division of an organization
	The federal government is divided into three *branches,* the executive, the judicial, and the legislative.
establish	to start
	It was her idea to *establish* a school for the blind.
implement	to carry out
	The Senate *implemented* the new procedure for voting.

The Three Branches of the U.S. Government

Executive - *President*
Enforces laws. Appoints officers. Makes treaties. Appoints Supreme Court judges. Serves as commander in chief of the United States military.

Legislative - *Congress*
Passes laws. Approves treaties and appointments. Provides for and maintains the military. Collects taxes. Pays debts. Borrows and coins money. Regulates trade.

Judicial - *Courts*
Interprets laws and treaties.

Words to Remember	
enact	to pass a law The city council met to *enact* a law on gun control.
executive	someone who runs things and sees that the people under him or her do their jobs; a manager She was a top *executive* with the telephone company.
recommendation	a statement saying something is a good idea The President made a *recommendation* to Congress on a law he hoped the Congress would pass.

The Constitution established the duties and powers of the two parts of Congress. For example, the Constitution gave Congress the power to collect taxes, pay debts, and provide money for the operation and defense of the country.

In Article Two, the Constitution established the **executive** branch of the government under a President. This individual would be commander in chief of the armed forces. The President would actually run the government according to the wishes of Congress. The President could not make laws. He or she could only recommend laws he or she would like to see **enacted** and ask the Congress to make such laws. The Congress would decide what to do with these **recommendations**.

The System of Checks and Balances

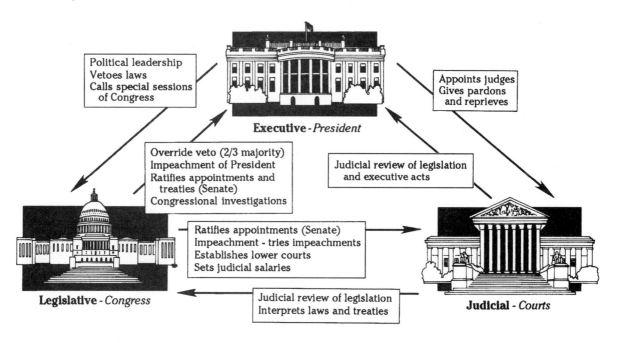

Political leadership
Vetoes laws
Calls special sessions of Congress

Appoints judges
Gives pardons and reprieves

Executive - *President*

Override veto (2/3 majority)
Impeachment of President
Ratifies appointments and treaties (Senate)
Congressional investigations

Judicial review of legislation and executive acts

Ratifies appointments (Senate)
Impeachment - tries impeachments
Establishes lower courts
Sets judicial salaries

Legislative - *Congress*

Judicial - *Courts*

Judicial review of legislation
Interprets laws and treaties

The President was given many duties. He or she could "veto" any bills Congress passed. This means that the President could say "No" to Congress when it passed a bill he or she did not approve of. Congress could still pass a bill over a veto, but two-thirds of the members of each part of the Congress had to vote against the veto for this to happen. This is important to our system of checks and balances.

Article Three of the Constitution established the **judicial** branch of the government. It said Congress could establish the court system in this country and set forth the duties of these courts. It created the United States Supreme Court and placed it on top of the judicial system.

Every case does not go to the Supreme Court. The chart on page 15 illustrates how a case can reach the Supreme Court.

The President of the United States appoints the members of the Supreme Court. Their term is for life, or until they decide to retire. Currently the Court has nine justices. One justice serves as the chief justice.

The Supreme Court does not make law, but it has a powerful **influence** on the law. The Court's main duty is to decide if a particular law passed by a state or by the U.S. Congress is permitted by the Constitution.

For example, suppose that a state has passed a law that makes it illegal for anyone to attend a Baptist church. The Supreme Court would study the Constitution. The members would see that under the First Amendment to the Constitution, everyone in this country has freedom of religion. The members of the Supreme Court would then vote on whether that state law is legal or **illegal** under the Constitution. Any law found to be illegal under the Constitution is said to be unconstitutional. If a law is unconstitutional, it ceases to be a law.

	Words to Remember
illegal	something that is against the law It is *illegal* to rob a bank.
influence	to change something by the power you might have over someone else He used his *influence* with the governor to get a law passed.
judicial	the duty of judging cases brought to court The judge had the *judicial* duty to decide which side in the case was right.

Path to the Supreme Court

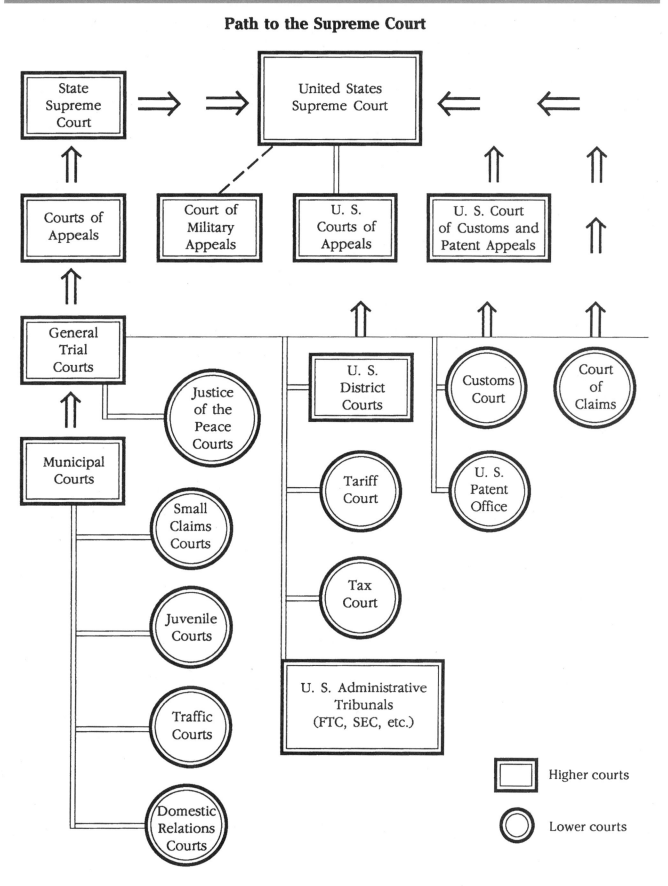

Review Unit 2

A Write the letter of the best answer on the line.

_____ 1. Where can you find your "rights" listed?
   a. in the Supreme Court
   b. in the Declaration of Independence
   c. in the Constitution

_____ 2. The United States has a form of government called a _____.
   a. dictatorship
   b. democracy
   c. monopoly

_____ 3. The most important court in the United States is the _____.
   a. circuit court
   b. Supreme Court
   c. juvenile court

_____ 4. You can attend any church you want to, according to the _____.
   a. First Amendment
   b. Second Amendment
   c. Third Amendment

_____ 5. The system of one branch of government watching over another branch of government is called the _____.
   a. grading system
   b. system of checks and balances
   c. operating system

B Find each word in bold type in the text. Think what the word means in that sentence. Then match the word to its definition by writing the correct letter on the line provided.

_____ 1. enact   a. to put into effect

_____ 2. influence   b. administration of justice

_____ 3. judicial   c. not acceptable by law

_____ 4. illegal   d. rules to follow

_____ 5. constitution   e. to affect or alter a decision

_____ 6. develop   f. to start

_____ 7. establish   g. something that is said to be a good idea

_____ 8. recommendation h. to promote the growth of something by steps

C Each of the following statements is *false.* Rewrite the statement correctly in the space provided.

1. The thirteen colonies declared their independence from Spain.

_____

_____

2. A democracy is run by one person.

_____

_____

3. The three branches of government are judicial, legislative, and presidential.

_____

_____

4. The President can make any law he or she wants.

_____

_____

5. The system of checks and balances ensures a balanced checking account.

_____

_____

6. The Congress can override any of the President's vetoes if only the House of Representatives agrees.

_____

_____

7. All laws come from the Supreme Court.

_____

_____

8. A Supreme Court justice is an elected official.

_____

_____

9. The Constitution has eight articles that provide the plan for the American government.

_____

_____

D Use the words in the box to complete the following sentences.

coin	Congress	executive	goal
judicial	legislative	republic	separation of powers
Supreme Court	treaties	vetoing	unconstitutional

1. The first article of the Constitution established the _____ branch of government.

2. Nine justices currently sit on the _____.

3. A _____ is a democracy in which citizens elect people to represent them in the government.

4. The division of the government into three branches is known

   as the _____.

5. The House of Representatives and the Senate make up the _____.

6. The President of the United States heads up the _____ branch of government.

7. The President can check the power of the Congress by _____ a bill it has passed.

8. The federal courts make up the _____ branch of the government.

9. The Supreme Court can determine that a law is _____.

10. Protecting individuals from the government was an important _____ of the writers of the Constitution.

11. One duty of the President is to make _____.

12. The Congress can borrow and _____ money.

The Bill of Rights

It is better, so the Fourth Amendment teaches, that the guilty sometimes go free than that citizens be subject to an easy arrest.
—William O. Douglas

Words to Remember

assemble   meet together
The people were told to *assemble* at city hall.

petition   to ask, usually in writing, for something
The crowd *petitioned* the governor for a change in the law.

practice   to do the same thing a lot, so as to become good at it; to do or perform customarily
The coach told Jim he should *practice* his basketball shots.
They wanted to *practice* their own religion.

The creators of the Constitution wanted every citizen of the United States to be treated fairly. They added ten amendments to the Constitution. These ten additions are called the *Bill of Rights.* Many of our rights as citizens are identified in the Bill of Rights.

First Amendment

The First Amendment is one of the most important parts of the Constitution. This amendment says there shall be no law made against freedom of religion, freedom of speech, or freedom of the press. It also says that the people of this country have the right to **assemble** peacefully. The people can **petition** the government to change its ways if those ways are not in agreement with what the people want.

The following are explanations of the parts of the First Amendment:

➤ Freedom of Religion

Many colonists came to America from Europe because they wanted to **practice** their own religion. In many European countries, there was an official state religion. At the time, the state religion in England was the Church of England. Those who did not follow that state religion were sometimes punished.

In the 1600s, many people who did not follow the rules of the Church of England came to North America. The Puritans set up a colony in Massachusetts. There they set up a religious state for people who wanted to live a simple life following Puritan teachings. Maryland was set up as a place where Roman Catholics could freely practice their faith. William Penn, a Quaker by faith, set up Pennsylvania as a colony. There people who believed in God could follow any religion they wished.

The **authors** of the U.S. Constitution did not want a state religion. The First Amendment says that Congress cannot establish a government religion. It also says that people can **worship** as they please. That means people can **attend** any church they want to. It also means that people do not have to practice any religion if they choose not to. The government cannot interfere. This is what is called *separation of church and state.*

➤*Freedom of Assembly*

Dr. Martin Luther King, Jr., helped lead a struggle for **civil rights** in the 1960s through speeches and protest marches. Dr. King had no power to make or change laws. He wanted to bring the wrongs that he thought were being committed in some states to the attention of the whole country. In effect, he was petitioning the government to change its ways. He wanted the government to give African-American citizens and other minorities their rights. Rights were promised to everyone according to the Constitution of the United States.

Dr. King was successful. Many changes were made because of his speeches, writings, and marches. He and his supporters used their right to peacefully assemble. They also used the right to ask the government to change its ways.

The Vietnam peace marchers during the late 1960s and early 1970s took advantage of these same rights. Hundreds of thousands of people linked arms and marched on Washington, D.C., the nation's capital, to protest the war in Vietnam. In part because of public pressure, the United States withdrew its armed forces from Vietnam.

➤*Freedom of Petition*

The usual way to petition the government is to collect on paper the names and addresses of people who support a particular cause. The proposal and signatures are then submitted to the government for action.

Words to Remember	
attend	go to The family always tried to *attend* church on Sunday.
author	someone who writes something, or who starts something The *author* of that book was John Jones. He was the *author* of the idea that people would never fly.
civil rights	the rights of a citizen The Constitution guarantees the *civil rights* of all citizens.
worship	to honor and to pay respect to a higher power All churches are places of *worship.*

In California, Howard Jarvis thought his taxes were too high. He was convinced that the state government was spending too much money. He asked the residents of California to sign a petition that would put the question of taxation on the ballot for the next election. The laws of California required a large number of signatures for a petition. Jarvis got the required number of signatures. In the next election, voters passed a law known as Proposition 13. Howard Jarvis and Paul Gann were the authors of Proposition 13. The law required California to put a limit on the increase in taxes each year.

▶ *Freedom of Speech and of the Press*
The First Amendment to the Constitution says that individuals have a right to freedom of speech and freedom of the press (newspapers, books, magazines, television). This amendment was established in protest against European monarchs. In many of the countries ruled by monarchs, the citizens could not complain about the government without the risk of going to jail.

In this country, citizens can complain about issues. They are protected from **prosecution** by the Constitution. However, no one can threaten the President, or anyone else, with bodily harm without risking a jail sentence. Criminal acts are not protected by the Constitution.

People can write almost anything they want. However, they have to be careful that they do not commit a criminal, or libelous act. **Libel** occurs when someone writes, for example, that a person is a thief and a liar. If the writer is sued by that person, he or she must prove in court that what was written is true. If the statement cannot be proven, then damages might be **assessed**. A **penalty** must be paid to the person who was insulted. In some cases, people can even go to jail for libeling someone. This is called *criminal libel*. **Slander** is the same as libel, except that slander is spoken while libel is written.

	Words to Remember
assess	put a tax or a fine on
	The store owner was *assessed* an amount of $200.00 for insulting a customer.
libel	unfavorable statements written about a person
	The reporter was accused of *libel* because of an article he wrote about a person.
penalty	punishment
	The *penalty* for speeding is a $30 fine.
prosecute	to bring legal action against someone and continue it
	The state has decided to *prosecute* the case against the bank robber.
slander	false charges that are spoken and damage another's reputation
	It is now up to a jury to decide whether what the actor said about his costar was *slander*.

You have looked at the First Amendment of the Bill of Rights. What are the others? The following list identifies the rights and protections in the first ten amendments to the Constitution.

The Bill of Rights

1. Freedom of religion, speech, the press, assembly, and petition
2. Right to keep arms in a militia
3. No forced housing of soldiers
4. Protection against unreasonable searches or taking of property
5. Right of due process of the law
6. Rights of people accused of crimes
7. Right to a jury trial in civil cases
8. Protection against unreasonable bail and cruel and unusual punishments
9. Protection of rights of the people not listed in the Constitution
10. Powers of the states and the people

Second and Third Amendments

The Second Amendment says that because a state needs a militia, people have the right to bear arms. The Third Amendment states that citizens cannot be forced to house military personnel in their homes during peacetime. They may have to do so during a war, but only as outlined in law.

Fourth Amendment

Amendments Four, Five, Six, and Eight involve the rights of a person accused of a crime. They were written so that persons accused or suspected of a crime are protected from unfair treatment. The Fourth Amendment **declares** that a person's home cannot be **invaded** by the government without proper cause and procedure. Procedure, in this case, is the steps the law must follow before a police officer can enter a house without permission. For example, if the police suspect someone of committing a crime and want to come into that person's house to search for evidence, they cannot go in without the permission of a court. This permission is called a **warrant**. An example of a warrant is on page 23. (Search and seizure is discussed in Unit 8.) A warrant is signed by a judge, and is one of the most important pieces of paper in criminal law.

Words to Remember	
declare	say strongly I *declare* myself as a candidate for President.
invade	get inside of During World War II, Germany *invaded* Poland.
warrant	a piece of paper that gives the holder legal permission to do something The judge signed the *warrant* permitting the police officer to search the house.

SEARCH AND SEIZURE WARRANT

_____COUNTY

TO: _____, Maryland State Police

or any other Maryland State Police Officer.

Greetings:

WHEREAS, it appears to me, the subscriber,_____,
Judge of the District Court,_____ County,
State of Maryland, by the written information of the affiant, hereinafter named, there is probable cause to
believe a crime is being committed, and the laws relating to the illegal manufacturing, distribution, and
possession of Controlled Dangerous Substances, as defined in Article 27, Sections 286 and 287, of the
Annotated Code of Maryland, 1957 Edition, as amended and revised dealing generally with Controlled
Dangerous Substances, including narcotics, hallucinogenic, and dangerous drugs, are being violated in
and upon a certain property and residence located at_____
_____. Said
property and residence is more particularly described as a_____
_____.

Furthermore, the said apartment can be positively identified by your affiant, _____.

And I am satisfied there is probable cause to believe there is now being concealed certain property,
namely Controlled Dangerous Substances, Packaging Materials, Monies, Records, and related Paraphernalia on the person(s), premises, and vehicle(s) described above, and the foregoing grounds for application for issuance of a Search and Seizure Warrant exist and is attached hereto and made part hereof.

The name of affiant is: _____, of the Maryland State Police,
Criminal Investigation Section, Security Barrack.

You are, therefore, hereby commanded, with the necessary and proper assistance to:

A. Enter and search the person(s), premises, and vehicle as completely described above;
B. Search the person(s) and clothing of_____, and all other person(s) found in or upon said premises and vehicle(s) who may be participating in violation of the statutes hereinbefore cited; and who may be concealing evidence, paraphernalia, and Controlled Dangerous Substances;
C. Open and search any safes, boxes, bags, compartments, or things in the nature thereof, found in or upon said premises or person(s) and vehicle(s).
D. Seize all evidence, paraphernalia, controlled dangerous substances, and money used in or incidental to the conduct or operation of Controlled Dangerous Substances violations, found in or upon said premises, person(s) and vehicle(s);
E. Books, records, receipts, notes, ledgers, and other papers relating to the transportation, ordering, purchasing, and distribution of Controlled Substances, in particular, Glutethimide and Acetaminophen #4, a Schedule III, Controlled Dangerous Substance;
F. Photographs, in particular, photographs of co-conspirators, of assets, and/or of Controlled Dangerous Substances;
G. Indicia of occupancy, residency, and/or ownership of the premises described in the affidavit, including, but not limited to, utility and telephone bills, canceled envelopes, etc.;
H. Arrest all person(s) found in or upon said premises, and vehicles who may be participating in violations of the statutes hereinbefore cited; and,
I. Bring said person(s), evidence, and paraphernalia before me, the subscriber, or some Judge of the State of Maryland, in and for the County aforesaid, to be dealt with and disposed of according to law.

HEREOF, fail not at your peril and have you then and there this Warrant.

GIVEN under my hand this _____ day of _____, in the year of Our Lord, 19___.

_____
Judge

To understand the rights guaranteed by the Fourth Amendment, consider the example of someone who stole a television set from a store. This person then took the television home and hid it. However, someone else saw this happen and told the store owner. The store owner calls the police. A warrant is "sworn out" for this person's arrest. That is, the store owner swears that the television was stolen and is now located in a certain house. The house address must be on the warrant. The stolen article must be described in the warrant.

A judge then studies the accusations and decides if forced entry into the house is proper under the law. If the judge thinks it is proper, he or she signs the warrant. The police can then demand entrance to the house. If the person inside the house refuses to open the door, then the police have the right to force their way in to look for the stolen TV set.

The only time a police officer can go into a house without a warrant is when there is "clear and present danger" to life. If a house is on fire and people are inside, a police officer has the right to come in and try to rescue them.

Fifth Amendment

Amendment Five prevents a government, whether city, state or federal, from keeping a person in jail without following due process. *Due process* means the same as *procedure.* In many countries, past and present, governments could have people put in jail or even killed without giving them a reason.

This amendment says that no one can be held to answer for a crime (except for small violations of the law) without being **indicted** by a **grand jury.** The grand jury process protects an innocent person from going to jail.

Words to Remember	
grand jury	a group of people who hear accusations of a crime, look at the evidence of the crime, and decide if the accused should be tried
	If the *grand jury* believes that a crime has been committed, it will file an indictment, and the accused person will have to stand trial. The *grand jury* process helps protect an innocent person from going to trial.
indicted	enough evidence is presented to the jury saying a certain person has committed a crime
	The truck driver was *indicted* on reckless-driving charges.

Constitutional Protections for the Accused

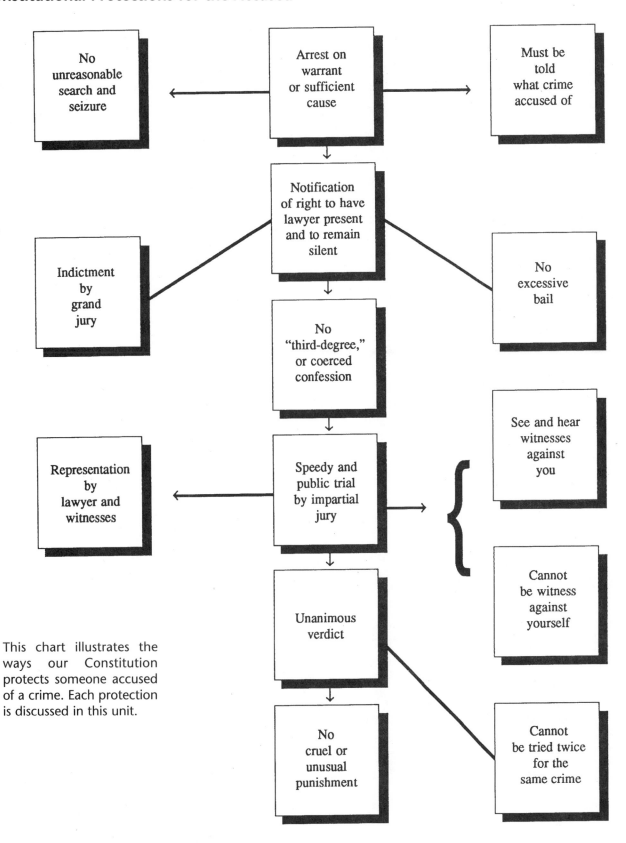

This chart illustrates the ways our Constitution protects someone accused of a crime. Each protection is discussed in this unit.

Boxes in the chart:
- No unreasonable search and seizure
- Arrest on warrant or sufficient cause
- Must be told what crime accused of
- Notification of right to have lawyer present and to remain silent
- Indictment by grand jury
- No excessive bail
- No "third-degree," or coerced confession
- Representation by lawyer and witnesses
- Speedy and public trial by impartial jury
- See and hear witnesses against you
- Cannot be witness against yourself
- Unanimous verdict
- No cruel or unusual punishment
- Cannot be tried twice for the same crime

Members of a grand jury examine all of the facts in the case. If the grand jury decides there is enough evidence that a certain person has committed a crime, it returns an indictment (a written, formal accusation) that permits the government to take the accused to trial.

The Fifth Amendment also says that a person cannot be tried twice for the same crime. For example, say that a person has been accused of stealing a car. He or she is indicted and stands trial in court. If found innocent of stealing that car, the person can never be forced to stand trial again for that particular theft. If that person is accused of stealing another car, however, the accused must stand trial for that event.

The Fifth Amendment protects people from being forced to **testify** against themselves. Suppose that you have been accused of a crime. You are in court and on the witness stand. A lawyer asks you, "Did you know that bank was going to be robbed?" If you say "Yes," a jury might think that you were part of the crime. You cannot be forced to answer that question because it might **incriminate** you. The makers of the Constitution put this in the Fifth Amendment because they were afraid that people accused of a crime would be threatened, or even beaten, to make them testify against themselves.

Sometimes in court, a witness will plead the "Fifth." Pleading the "Fifth" means that the witness is exercising his or her right not to answer a question that might make him or her appear to be involved in the crime. The person may say, "I refuse to answer that question on the grounds that it may tend to incriminate me." Saying these words does not mean the person is guilty. It just means that the person chooses not to answer the question.

Finally, the Fifth Amendment says the government cannot take property away from people without fair **compensation**. For example, suppose that a city wants to build a road. The road is supposed to go right through the center of a house. The city has the right to tear down the house and build the road, but it must pay the owner what the house and land are worth.

Words to Remember	
compensation	payment, often in money The worker received *compensation* for injuries received on the job.
incriminate	show that one is involved in a crime The evidence *incriminated* the accused.
testify	give evidence under oath Three witnesses were called to *testify* against the accused.

Words to Remember	
impartial	doesn't care which side wins The jury heard both sides of the argument and made an *impartial* decision.
juror	member of a jury The twelve *jurors* listened carefully to the witnesses.
peers	persons equal to one another The accused has the right to a trial by a jury of *peers.*

Sixth Amendment

The Sixth Amendment provides for (1) a speedy and public trial, and (2) an **impartial** jury for anyone accused of a crime. Although the accused has the right to a trial by a jury of **peers,** he or she can refuse a jury trial and ask for the case to be heard and decided by a judge. If the accused chooses a jury trial, **jurors** are selected from a pool of citizens called for jury duty. The judge and lawyers ask the potential (possible) jurors questions. They are looking for jurors who will pay close attention to the trial proceedings and who will make a fair, thoughtful decision.

The amendment also says that the accused has to be told exactly what the charges are against him or her. The accused or his or her lawyer must be allowed to question any witnesses against him or her in court.

The amendment says that the accused has a right to present favorable witnesses (people who would take the side of the accused). The person accused has the right to be represented by a lawyer in court. If the accused cannot afford to hire a lawyer, one will be given to him or her free of charge.

Refer to the stolen television set that was discussed earlier in the chapter. A man stole it from a store and hid it in his house. That person has been indicted by a grand jury for the theft and is now standing trial. That is, he is in court before a judge and jury, who will try to figure out whether he is guilty or innocent.

The law states that the accused must get a speedy and public trial. If there were no Sixth Amendment, police could put this person in jail and forget about him. A person could stay in jail for a long time and be entirely innocent of any crime. That would be unfair.

	Word to Remember
bail	the sum of money that a person accused of a crime has to give to the court if he or she wants to stay out of jail until the trial is held *Bail* was set at $5,000.

In some states, an accused person must be tried within 180 days. If not, that person is released and the charges are dropped, even if the charge is a serious one, like murder. In other states, an accused person must be tried sooner than that. The rules differ from state to state.

An accused person must also get a public trial. This protects the accused person. He or she cannot be tried by a court in secret. Anyone can watch the trial, and it can be reported in the news.

Eighth Amendment

The Eighth Amendment states that the amount of a person's **bail** shall be fair and related to the nature of the crime. The amendment also guarantees that persons found guilty of a crime shall not receive "cruel and unusual punishment."

Refer again to the stolen television set. The person accused of stealing the set would be brought before a judge. The judge would set bail according to the seriousness of the crime. In the case of the television, bail might be set at $2,500.

The court would hold the bail money until a trial was held and the accused person was found guilty or innocent. Either way, the bail money is returned to the accused. Bail money is given to the court to help make sure that the accused shows up for his trial. If the accused does not show up for the trial, he loses the bail money and the judge issues a warrant for his arrest. If the accused cannot afford to put up bail, or doesn't want to, then that person must stay in jail until his trial for stealing the TV is held.

Excessive bail means a sum of money the court demands that is far greater than the seriousness of the crime. For example, if bail in the case of the stolen TV set were set at $100,000 instead of $2,500, it would be considered excessive. The accused or his lawyer could ask for a reduction in the amount of the bail. They could mention the Eighth Amendment as a reason.

Cruel and unusual punishment is self-explanatory. If a person is found guilty of stealing a TV set, he might be sentenced to a year in jail. Employees of the jail cannot hang this person by his thumbs, or make the person stay out in the cold weather all night. These would be cruel and unusual punishments.

In some states, judges have ruled that there are too many prisoners in their jails (this is called *overcrowding*). They have said that this is cruel and unusual punishment. They have given their states three choices: build more jails, enlarge the ones they have, or let some of the prisoners go free.

Other Amendments in the Bill of Rights
You have now read about all but three amendments in the Bill of Rights. The Seventh Amendment addresses civil cases. Civil cases are lawsuits. This amendment states that parties in a lawsuit may ask for a jury trial if the amount of money involved is more than $20.00.

It also states that the jury's decision cannot be overturned simply because a judge disagrees with it. It can be overturned, however, if points of law are questioned.

The Ninth Amendment states that the people have rights other than those listed in the Constitution. This amendment recognizes that the Constitution could not possibly list all of the rights of citizens.

The Constitution gives the federal government certain powers. It also denies some powers to the states, such as the power to coin money. The Tenth Amendment notes that any powers not given to the federal government or denied to the states belong to the states or to the people.

The amendments in the Bill of Rights help protect the rights and freedoms of citizens. Together they identify the rights of individuals, the rights of people accused of crimes, and protections from abuses by the government.

More Amendments
The ten amendments in the Bill of Rights were proposed in 1789. They became part of the Constitution in 1791. Since the Bill of Rights was adopted, seventeen more amendments have been added to the Constitution over the years. The Constitution is now made up of seven "articles" and 27 amendments. These amendments include such things as the ending of slavery in the United States (Thirteenth Amendment); voting rights for all races (Fifteenth Amendment); voting rights for women (Nineteenth Amendment); and one of the more recent amendments, which set the voting age at 18 (Twenty-sixth Amendment).

	Word to Remember
confess	admit guilt
	My daughter *confessed* that she had lost her library book.
conflict	clash, differ
	The time of the game *conflicts* with my work schedule.
convict	prove guilty
	The jury *convicted* the accused of the crime.

State Constitutions

Each state of the union has its own constitution. These state constitutions are much like the U.S. Constitution. The United States is a country where people live under two separate constitutions.

State constitutions contain items of importance for that particular state. For example, a state constitution specifies the length of term of the governor of the state and determines when the state legislature meets (a state legislature is much like the U.S. Congress). State constitutions are usually longer and contain many more details than the Constitution of the United States. Like the Constitution, the state constitutions can also be amended. Over time, however, some states have chosen to write new constitutions. North Carolina and Illinois, for example, adopted new constitutions in the 1970s. Every state constitution must agree with the national Constitution, however. A state constitution cannot permit laws that the federal Constitution does not allow. For example, a state constitution cannot permit a law against freedom of speech because this **conflicts** with the Constitution.

The Miranda Rights

The Miranda Rights are different from the Bill of Rights. The Miranda Rights are a list of rights that an individual is entitled to if he or she is arrested. These rights are a result of a famous Supreme Court Case, *Miranda v. Arizona.*

Ernesto Miranda was arrested in 1963 on charges of kidnapping and rape. During questioning by the police, Miranda **confessed** to the crime. At his trial, Miranda's confession was used as evidence against him. He was **convicted** and sent to jail. Miranda appealed his case to the Supreme Court on the grounds that the police had not told him about his rights when they arrested him.

The Supreme Court heard Miranda's case and in 1966 ruled in his favor. The Court based its decision on the Fifth and Sixth Amendments to the Constitution. The Bill of Rights proved to be important to Miranda. His conviction was overturned. It is also important to others accused of crimes. In making its ruling, the Court said that the police must inform a person they arrest of his or her rights before they can question the person. See the following page for an official list of Miranda rights.

This is a copy of the official Miranda Rights.

CASE # _____

_____
Name of Person Being Interviewed

OHIO STATE POLICE
ADVICE OF MIRANDA RIGHTS

Date: _____   Place: _____

Time: _____   Person Explaining Rights: _____

You are now being questioned as to any information you may have pertaining to an official police investigation. Therefore, you are advised of the following rights:

1. You have the right to remain silent.
2. Anything you say or write may be used against you in a court of law.
3. You have the right to talk to a lawyer before answering any questions and to have a lawyer present at any time before or during questioning.
4. If you now want the assistance of a lawyer but cannot afford to hire one, you will not be asked any more questions at this time and you may request the court to appoint a lawyer for you without charge.
5. If you agree to answer questions, you may stop at any time and request the assistance of a lawyer, and no further questions will be asked of you.

I have read or have had read to me this explanation of my rights. I fully understand each of these rights and I am willing to answer questions without consulting a lawyer or having a lawyer present at this time. My decision to answer questions is entirely free and voluntary and I have not been promised anything nor have I been threatened or intimidated in any manner.

_____
(Signature)

Date: _____

Witnessed: _____

Review Unit 3

A Write the letter of the best answer on the line.

_____ 1. What is one freedom promised by the First Amendment?
   a. freedom to vote
   b. freedom of religion
   c. freedom of education

_____ 2. What is the usual way to petition the government?
   a. assemble outside the White House
   b. get the names and addresses of a lot of people on paper and give them to the government
   c. go around demanding your rights

_____ 3. When do you commit a libel?
   a. when you tell lies about people in writing
   b. when you cross the street in the middle of the block
   c. when you call someone a thief and a liar

_____ 4. What was being exercised when Dr. King and his followers held their marches?
   a. their right to have legal representation
   b. their right to peaceable assembly
   c. their right to overthrow the government

_____ 5. Without your agreement, a police officer must have a _____ to legally come into your home.
   a. document
   b. gun
   c. warrant

_____ 6. Whose legal rights do the Fourth, Fifth, Sixth, and Eighth Amendments protect?
   a. the judge
   b. the accused person
   c. the victim of a crime

_____ 7. What is an indictment?
   a. a bench in a courtroom
   b. a written, formal accusation of a crime
   c. a license to drive a car

_____ 8. What is one of the rights that the Sixth Amendment gives?
   a. the right to reasonable bail
   b. the right to free speech
   c. the right to a speedy and public trial

_____ 9. An accused person must have a _____ trial.

    a. long

    b. public

    c. secret

_____ 10. _____ is a sum of money an accused person must give to the court to stay out of jail until his or her trial.

    a. Loan

    b. Bail

    c. Mortgage

Understanding Your Rights

Certain words are often used in opinions. Words like *always, never, I think, I believe, best,* and *worst* are often clues that a statement is an opinion. The statement "I think the United States is the best country in the world" is an opinion.

B All the statements below concern your legal rights. Some statements are facts and others are opinions. Decide whether each statement is a fact or an opinion. Write the word *Fact* next to a statement that is a fact. Write the word *Opinion* next to a statement that is an opinion.

_____ 1. Your own lawyer is bound to be better than the lawyer the judge appoints you.

_____ 2. The police are required to tell you what your rights are.

_____ 3. Taxpayers should not have to pay for lawyers for people who can't afford one.

_____ 4. The law says you have the right to a lawyer whether you can afford one or not.

_____ 5. It is a good idea to make young people wait in jail until they come to trial instead of releasing them on bail.

_____ 6. The judge decides whether to set bail or release a person on his or her own recognizance (promise to return).

_____ 7. In a case in which everyone knows that the defendant is guilty, he or she should just be sent to jail without a trial.

_____ 8. Everyone is entitled to due process of the law.

_____ 9. If you lie to the police, you will always get into more trouble.

_____ 10. You do not have to tell the police anything except your name and address until you see a lawyer.

Guaranteed Rights

C Here are some true-to-life situations. Fill in the chart below with the basic right being protected in each situation. There may be more than one right involved. In the third column, write the number of the amendment that states this right.

1. Ted Johnson is arrested and charged with stealing $100. He does not have any money for a lawyer. He requests a lawyer to defend him. The government gives him a lawyer free of charge.

2. A political candidate who opposed the President speaks against the President at an outdoor political rally. Many people gather to listen.

3. Kim Parks criticizes the government for the high taxes she must pay. She feels the middle class is being cheated.

4. The *Evening Star* newspaper prints an editorial exposing corruption (illegal dealings) in government.

5. Martin Goldberg signs a petition to the government for stricter pollution controls in nuclear plants.

6. The Francos have been attending a certain church. They decide they are going to attend a different church next week.

Statement	Right	Amendment
1.		
2.		
3.		
4.		
5.		
6.		

Know Your Rights

D Study the list below. Refer to the Miranda Rights on page 31 and the chart on page 25. In the space provided, copy the eight statements that would apply if you are ever arrested.

If you are arrested, you

1. must give your name and address (identify yourself).

2. must not submit to fingerprinting.

3. must be told the charge and informed of your constitutional rights.

4. should try to resist arrest.

5. must sign a confession of guilt.

6. do not have to answer *all* questions.

7. may remain silent, except to give your name and address.

8. are entitled to a phone call to your family or lawyer.

9. should try to run away if you have not done anything.

10. have the right to have your bail set if you are being held.

11. may stop answering questions at any time.

12. have the right to know why you are being arrested.

_____

_____

_____

_____

_____

_____

_____

_____

_____

Review Units 1–3

A Write the letter of the best answer on the line.

_____ **1.** What two groups heavily influenced our current legal system?
   a. the Spanish and the French
   b. the Romans and the English
   c. the Greeks and the Chinese

_____ **2.** What does the law protect?
   a. individuals
   b. government
   c. police officers

_____ **3.** What did the Romans believe that we still believe today?
   a. A person is guilty until proven innocent.
   b. A person is guilty if he or she remains silent when questioned by the police.
   c. A person is innocent until proven guilty.

_____ **4.** What is the English common law based upon?
   a. the customs and habits of the Romans
   b. the customs and habits of the English
   c. the customs and habits of Americans

_____ **5.** Charges may be _____, if procedure is not followed.
   a. added
   b. more serious
   c. nullified

_____ **6.** Who runs a democracy?
   a. the government
   b. the people
   c. the police

_____ **7.** Why was the Constitution written?
   a. to provide for the existence of a dictatorship in the United States
   b. to develop a monarchy similar to the one that existed in England
   c. to provide for the protection of the individual from the government

_____ **8.** What did the first article of the Constitution establish?
   a. the presidency
   b. the Supreme Court
   c. the Congress

36   UNITS 1–3 *REVIEW*

_____ 9. What are the two houses of Congress?
  a. the House of Representatives and the Senate
  b. the Democratic House and the Republican House
  c. the House of Representatives and the Supreme Court

_____ 10. Who is the commander in chief of the armed forces?
  a. the Vice President
  b. the President
  c. the surgeon general

_____ 11. Laws are enacted by ____.
  a. the Supreme Court
  b. the Congress
  c. the President

_____ 12. Members of the Supreme Court preside ____.
  a. for a term of ten years
  b. only as long as the President who appointed them remains in office
  c. for life

_____ 13. What is the main duty of the Supreme Court?
  a. to decide if a particular law passed by a state or by the Congress is permitted by the Constitution
  b. to enact laws that are permitted by the Constitution
  c. to enact the particular laws requested by the Congress or by a state

_____ 14. The First Amendment provides for which of the following?
  a. freedom of speech
  b. freedom of dress
  c. freedom of movement

_____ 15. Congress will never establish a state religion because of the principle known as ____.
  a. separation of church and state
  b. religious supremacy
  c. governmental respect for religion

_____ 16. What type of acts are not protected under the First Amendment of the Constitution?
  a. anonymous acts
  b. criminal acts
  c. inappropriate acts

_____ 17. If James writes in the school newspaper that Maria is a thief and it is not true, then Maria can sue James for _____.

    a. slander

    b. libel

    c. assault

_____ 18. When can the police enter your house without a warrant and without your permission?

    a. when they decide that they have a right to enter your house

    b. when a neighbor gives permission for them to enter your house

    c. when there is a life-threatening situation inside your house

_____ 19. Under the Fifth Amendment, can a person be tried twice for the same crime if found innocent?

    a. yes

    b. no

    c. yes, under certain circumstances

_____ 20. What amendment requires the court to appoint a lawyer, free of charge, to someone accused of a crime?

    a. the Second Amendment

    b. the Fourth Amendment

    c. the Sixth Amendment

B Write the answers to the questions.

1. Why is the United States both a democracy and a republic?

_____

_____

_____

2. What right is guaranteed in the Seventh Amendment to the Constitution?

_____

_____

_____

3. How does the *Miranda* decision demonstrate the importance of police following proper procedures when arresting someone?

_____

_____

_____

_____

Types of Crimes

Crimes are not to be measured by the issue of events,
but from the bad intentions of men.
–Marcus Tallius Cicero

Words to Remember	
accomplice	person who helps out in a crime or a wrongdoing The bank robber's *accomplice* waited in the get-away car.
crime	something that can be punished under a law He got 20 years in jail for the *crime* of bank robbery.
felony	a crime that can be punished by more than one year in jail Bank robbery is a *felony,* for which you can be punished with up to 20 years in jail.
monetary	concerning money A basic *monetary* unit in the United States is the dollar.

A **crime** is an act that can be punished under a written law. Bank robbery is a crime because there are written laws against robbing banks. Crimes are generally divided into two classes—felonies and misdemeanors. **Monetary** value of the crime sometimes determines if the charge is a misdemeanor or a felony. The amount varies from state to state. For example, in Maryland, a misdemeanor is charged if a stolen item is worth less than $300.00.

A **felony** is the most serious type of criminal act. A felony usually includes a punishment of more than one year in jail, a fine, or both. Examples of felonies include forgery, selling narcotics, grand theft, and armed robbery. If a felony has been committed, the person who committed the crime can be punished under the law by going to jail. Some felonies, like murder, can be punished by death in some states.

Sometimes a person can be accused and convicted of a crime even though that person did not actually do it. For example, a man and a woman go into a store with the intent of robbing it. The woman has a gun, the man does not. During the robbery, the woman shoots and kills the store clerk. Both persons can be convicted of armed robbery. They can also be convicted of murder even though only one had a gun. The man is charged with being an accomplice. An **accomplice** is someone who takes part in a crime. Both persons could get the same penalty, even though only one of them shot the store clerk.

A **misdemeanor** is not as serious as a felony. A criminal misdemeanor usually carries a penalty of up to a year in jail, a fine, or both. Length of sentence depends on the seriousness of the crime. Examples of misdemeanors are petty theft and receiving stolen goods.

A **violation** does not carry a jail sentence and is not even a crime. If someone commits a violation, he or she has broken a rule and may have to pay a fine. Speeding is a violation, and the speeder can receive a fine.

A **petty** theft is when someone steals something of little value. For example, if someone is caught stealing a pair of $10.00 earrings, that person could be charged with petty theft. Grand theft is a serious crime. Someone who steals a car would be charged with grand theft.

It is important to know the difference between felonies, misdemeanors, and violations. If a judge decides that a felony has been committed, the accused has the right to a trial by jury. If he or she cannot afford a lawyer, then the state will provide that person with one.

A judge may decide that the seriousness of the crime does not require a jury. In that case, a judge decides the guilt or innocence of the violator. A lawyer can represent someone accused of a misdemeanor or a violation, but the individual will have to pay the legal fee. A jury trial can also be requested if the accused thinks he or she has a better chance of being **acquitted** by a jury than by the judge.

The chart on page 41 illustrates the stages of a criminal trial. The chart breaks down each stage and explains who is involved.

Words to Remember	
acquitted	freed of guilt, found not guilty The man charged with stealing was *acquitted* by the jury.
misdemeanor	a crime that can be punished with up to one year in jail Stealing a TV set is a *misdemeanor,* for which you can be punished with up to one year in jail.
petty	small Stealing the pocketbook was considered a *petty* crime.
violation	breaking of a rule; usually punished with a fine He was fined $40 for a speeding *violation.*

Stages in a Criminal Trial (Felony)			
Stage	**Agencies Involved**	**Action Taken**	**Other Possible Actions**
• *Apprehension*	Police Court may furnish warrants.	Investigation Apprehension Arrest Booking	Case dropped for insufficient evidence.
• *Indictment*	Magistrate Court Prosecuting attorney Grand Jury	Preliminary hearing Setting of bail Evidence considered by grand jury. Indictment handed down. Case placed on docket	Charges reduced. Case dismissed.
• *Trial*	General trial court	Arraignment Plea Jury selection Witnesses testify. Prosecution and defense argue the case. Jury returns a verdict.	Court accepts a lesser plea. Mistrial declared. Defendant acquitted. Appeal to higher court.
• *Sentencing*	General trial court State penal system	Judge and/or jury pronounces sentence: fine, imprisonment, or both. Sentence begins.	Suspended sentence Probation Pardon

Review Unit 4

A Write the letter of the best answer on the line.

_____ 1. What is a felony?
   a. the most serious type of crime
   b. the least serious type of crime
   c. a written, formal accusation of a crime

_____ 2. How much time might you have to spend in prison for committing a bank robbery?
   a. up to twenty years in jail
   b. up to ten years in jail
   c. up to five years in jail

_____ 3. A person accused of a felony has a right to trial by _____.
   a. a lawyer
   b. a jury
   c. the judge

_____ 4. An accomplice is one who takes part in a _____.
   a. crime
   b. violation
   c. trial

_____ 5. What is a speeding ticket listed as?
   a. a felony
   b. a misdemeanor
   c. a violation

_____ 6. An accused person who cannot afford a lawyer will be _____.
   a. sent home with a reprimand (warning)
   b. provided with one, free of charge
   c. put in prison until he or she can afford one

_____ 7. A person who helps commits a crime is known as an _____.
   a. felon
   b. accomplice
   c. petty thief

_____ 8. If an accused person is acquitted, that means that the person _____.
   a. is found not guilty
   b. can be retried
   c. is declared guilty

Name That Crime

 B Consider what you have learned about types of crimes. Now you have the chance to be an *officer* of the law. Read and evaluate each criminal act. Write the crime you would charge the person with.

Crime

- drunk driving
- homicide
- rape
- forgery
- armed robbery
- possession of controlled dangerous substances
- petty theft
- grand theft
- selling controlled dangerous substances
- receiving stolen goods

Criminal Act

_____ 1. Jessica Aarons had too much to drink at the party but insisted on driving home.

_____ 2. William Polaski kills his neighbor in a fight.

_____ 3. Roy Chen steals a car.

_____ 4. Kate Parks sells cocaine.

_____ 5. Anthony Evanston buys a stereo that was stolen.

_____ 6. Sandra Lewis is sexually assaulted by Cory Livingston.

_____ 7. Liz Clark finds Mrs. Ainsworth's checkbook on the bus and goes on a shopping spree. She signs Mrs. Ainsworth's name on the checks.

_____ 8. Dennis O'Hanlon is searched by the police. They find three ounces of cocaine on him.

_____ 9. Irma Sarkiss has stolen a package of eye shadow from Anthony's Department store.

_____ 10. Stephanie Munson uses a gun to hold up a bank.

_____ 11. Carson Jones steals a major artwork from the art museum.

_____ 12. Leslie Foster signs her name on a check written to her mother and keeps the money without permission.

Lawyer, Judge, and Jury

Although the law is a highly learned profession, we are well aware that it is an intensely practical one.
–Frederick M. Vension

Words to Remember	
client	customer The lawyer told his *client* he thought he could win the case.
confidential	secret or private A lawyer should not reveal *confidential* information provided by a client.
ethical	moral, proper To give the lost money back was the *ethical* thing to do.
participant	one who takes part He was a *participant* in the football game.
relationship	a connection You have a special *relationship* with your mother.

The Lawyer

The major **participants** in most criminal trials are the lawyers, the judge, and the jury. A lawyer is a person specially trained in school to practice law. A lawyer usually, but not always, has earned a college degree and then has attended law school. After graduation from law school, he or she has to take and pass an important test called a *state bar examination.*

There are several types of lawyers. Many lawyers never appear in a criminal court of law. They handle deeds (a paper that proves that an individual owns certain property, like a house), wills (a paper that provides for distribution of money and property when someone dies), and other legal papers. They may work for a corporation and handle the corporation's legal matters. Some lawyers handle only income tax cases. Others handle only civil suits. Civil cases will be explained later in this book. Criminal lawyers usually handle only criminal cases.

A lawyer's role is to defend his or her **client** or protect his or her client's interests in a legal and **ethical** way. Anything a client tells a lawyer is **confidential.**

A client's right to confidential discussions with his or her attorney is known as attorney-client privilege. This means that anything a client tells his or her lawyer confidentially, the lawyer may not tell anyone else. There are cases in which the attorney-client privilege does not apply. For example, if a client reveals that he or she is about to commit a crime, his or her lawyer is not responsible for maintaining confidentiality. Too, if a lawyer is sued by a client, the attorney may reveal communications with the client.

Three Kinds of Lawyers

Attorney-at-law is another term for a lawyer. An attorney is trained to represent people in lawsuits and other legal matters. Lawyers specialize in specific areas of law. Three types of lawyers are described below.

The Corporate Lawyer—This lawyer is usually employed by a specific corporation. He or she specializes in legal matters that are important to his or her company. For example, a lawyer who is employed by a publishing company would be very knowledgeable about copyright laws, royalty contracts, etc.

The Family Lawyer—A family lawyer helps and advises members of his or her community in matters that affect their lives. A family lawyer would be used to write a personal will, buy a house, or represent his or her client in divorce proceedings.

The Criminal Lawyer—Any person accused of a crime has the right to be represented in the courts. Criminal laws are very complicated. A corporate lawyer or a family lawyer is seldom familiar enough with these laws to adequately represent someone. A criminal lawyer specializes in criminal laws.

As noted on page 44, a lawyer cannot tell a friend what an accused person has told him or her about a case. He or she does not have to tell a judge or jury what an accused person has said to him or her. This is one way the lawyer helps protect his or her client.

Corporate Lawyer

Family Lawyer

Criminal Lawyer

Recently, in Florida, a man was struck and killed by a car while walking along a highway. The driver of the car left the scene of the accident without telling anyone he had struck someone with his car. The next day, the driver of the car went to see a lawyer and told him that he thought he had struck someone the night before. The police wanted to know the name of the driver. The lawyer would not give the police the name. The police could not force the lawyer to give them the client's name because of the special **relationship** between lawyer and client.

Another way a lawyer protects his or her client's interests is when selecting a jury for the client's trial. The lawyer has the right to question jurors to see if they are fair-minded. For example, he or she might ask a juror if the juror likes or dislikes farmers. If the accused is a farmer, and the juror says he or she doesn't like farmers, then the lawyer has the right to ask the judge to excuse that juror. That juror is sent home and another person takes his or her place. This is called a *challenge.*

Lawyers charge money for their services. Their fees vary depending on what charges they are defending. Fees should be determined before retaining (hiring) a lawyer. It is a good idea to contact several lawyers and compare their fees. Some lawyers charge by the hour. This is usually done when a lawyer doesn't know how long it is going to take to defend the case. Most lawyers want a sum of money before they will take a case. This is called a *retainer fee,* and it is like a down payment.

The Judge
Judges are elected or appointed to this position on the basis of their knowledge of the law and their standing in the community. Becoming a judge is a high honor in our society. Members of the United States Supreme Court are appointed by the President of the United States.

The judge plays an important role in the courtroom. In a criminal trial, the judge protects the public's interest. The judge sees that the trial is orderly and fair to both sides.

The two opposing forces are the defendant (the person accused of the crime), and the prosecutor (the person representing the state) who believes the defendant is guilty and wants to put him or her in jail.

The Jury
The jury system began in England hundreds of years ago. It has continued because it is the fairest system for deciding guilt or innocence. In a jury system, **evidence** is presented to an impartial jury by the state. The state is supposed to prove that a certain person has committed a crime.

Word to Remember	
evidence	something (a gun, a stolen television set, fingerprints, etc.) that tends to prove something
	The prosecutor presented as *evidence* a gun with the accused person's fingerprints on it.

	Words to Remember
hung jury	a jury that cannot agree on a verdict
	The foreman of the jury informed the judge that it was a *hung jury*.
summons	an order to appear
	Terrell received a *summons* to appear in the jury pool room at 9 o'clock Monday morning.

The accused person and the state have the right to call witnesses and present evidence supporting their side. The two opponents then argue the case before the judge and jury.

The final decision on the guilt or innocence of the accused is up to the jury. There are usually twelve jury members in a criminal trial. All twelve must agree on the verdict for the accused to be convicted. This is determined by a vote of the jury. If only one person does not believe that the accused is guilty, the jury reports that fact to the judge. This is called a **hung jury**. If this happens, the charges against the accused can be dismissed. The state can try to get a new trial. With a new trial, everything starts all over again at a later date and with a different jury.

Members of a jury are picked from a jury pool made up of citizens. The citizens in the pool are picked for jury duty in different ways: from voting lists, tax rolls, or driver's license lists. People chosen for a jury pool often receive a letter informing them that they have been chosen. The letter may include a questionnaire that asks about work and any situations that may prevent the person from serving on a jury. The citizen may later receive a **summons** ordering the citizen to appear on a certain date and time in the jury pool room. Any citizen might be called to serve on a jury. It is very difficult to be excused from jury duty. For example, a person has to be seriously ill, or prove to the court that his or her business cannot run without him or her for a certain period of time. If a summons to serve on a jury is ignored, the person can be fined or even jailed. Jury duty is regarded as a responsibility for all citizens. The system of justice would not work without it.

The letter of page 48 is an example of a jury summons letter. It explains what the potential jury member should do and how much the juror will be reimbursed.

A Summons to Appear for Jury Duty

The Circuit Court for
Gwinnett County
Norcross, Georgia
(401) 555-1111

March 1, 1990

James P. Hargus
221 Maple Way
Norcross, Georgia

    You have been selected to serve on the _____ Term Petit Jury for Gwinnett County. You are on call for the month of _____ . Please be available to report to the County Courts Building, Norcross, Georgia. A letter will be sent to you, a few days prior to your reporting time, explaining your reporting procedure. You will, at that time, be given a juror number and a telephone number to call explaining whether you should or should not report on _____ . If you do not report on that date, you will continue to call everyday after 4 p.m. for the following day's schedule.

    Your service will be for the calendar month of _____ . You will be paid fifteen dollars for each day of your appearance plus twelve cents per mile for each mile traveled between home and court.

    If unable to serve during the assigned month, the Jury Commissioner must be advised in writing by _____ . Medical excuses require doctor's certification. All requests for date changes must be signed by you and addressed to Richard Lewis, Jury Commissioner.

Very truly yours,

(Signature)

Jury Judge

FC:lb

Review Unit 5

Write the letter of the best answer on the line.

_____ 1. What is the first thing a person should think of when accused?
   a. leaving town
   b. getting a lawyer
   c. calling a judge

_____ 2. Who can a lawyer talk to about what a client has said to him or her?
   a. a judge
   b. his best friend
   c. no one

_____ 3. A lawyer's role is to defend his or her _____.
   a. honor
   b. ethics
   c. client

_____ 4. A person accused of a crime has the right to get a _____.
   a. lawyer
   b. warrant
   c. violation

_____ 5. What does someone have to pass in order to practice law?
   a. a final exam
   b. school boards
   c. the state bar examination

_____ 6. Who appoints members of the United States Supreme Court?
   a. the governors
   b. the mayors
   c. the President

_____ 7. Who makes the final decision on guilt or innocence?
   a. the judge
   b. the prosecutor
   c. the jury

_____ 8. A judge is almost always a _____.
   a. defendant
   b. client
   c. lawyer

R
E
V
I
E
W

_____ **9.** The judge is in court to protect the _____ interests.
   a. public's
   b. lawyer's
   c. jury's

_____ **10.** Who are the opposing (against each other) forces in a trial?
   a. the prosecutor and the defendant
   b. the judge and the jury
   c. the prosecutor and the judge

_____ **11.** Where did our jury system begin?
   a. in France
   b. in England
   c. in the United States

_____ **12.** How many people are usually on a jury?
   a. twelve
   b. nine
   c. eight

_____ **13.** Evidence is presented to an _____ jury.
   a. industrious
   b. impartial
   c. unconscious

_____ **14.** The accused and the state have the right to call _____.
   a. a lawyer
   b. witnesses
   c. home

_____ **15.** A hung jury is one in which _____.
   a. every jury member agrees on the verdict
   b. one or every jury member has a different opinion
   c. every jury member agrees with the judge

_____ **16.** You would most likely ask a _____ to draw up a will.
   a. corporate lawyer
   b. family lawyer
   c. criminal lawyer

50   UNIT 5 *REVIEW*

The Court System

We, like the eagles, were born to be free. Yet we are obliged,
in order to live at all, to make a cage of laws for ourselves
and to stand on the perch.
–William Bolitho

Words to Remember	
civil suit	a legal action brought by one party against another to recover damages for a wrong Mr. Roucker filed a *civil suit* against the car dealer who cheated him out of his money.
warranty	promise to repair or pay for repairs The car had a 5-year or 5,000-mile *warranty* on engine parts.

There are many more **civil suits** in the courts than there are criminal cases. *Civil* means "private," or belonging to an individual. A person will file a civil suit because he or she thinks he or she has been wronged by someone else. He or she wants to collect money and/or property from a person who wronged him or her. A civil suit is a way to peacefully settle an argument between two parties. Otherwise, disagreements might be settled with fist fights. The following story illustrates a civil suit.

A man named Richard Roucker bought a used 1984 blue Cadillac from a car dealer. The Cadillac had only 25,000 miles on the odometer. Mr. Roucker paid the car dealer $15,000 for the Cadillac and drove it home.

Several weeks later, the engine developed a noise, and Mr. Roucker took the car to a repair shop. A mechanic looked at the engine and found the trouble. The mechanic called General Motors, the maker of the Cadillac, to see if the car was still covered by a **warranty.** A car warranty is a promise by the maker of the car to pay for damaged parts.

The representative at General Motors looked at the company records. The records showed that the Cadillac had been repaired the year before for the same problem. Someone had asked questions at that time about a warranty. The records showed the Cadillac had had 98,000 miles on the odometer when it was first reported. The car was no longer covered by a warranty.

The odometer had been turned back on Mr. Roucker's Cadillac. Mr. Roucker had been cheated. He had paid a high price for the car because he thought it had only 25,000 miles on it. In truth, the car had far more than 25,000 miles on it.

Mr. Roucker went back to the car dealer and complained. The car dealer said she did not know anything about the changed odometer. She refused to take the Cadillac back. Mr. Roucker went to a lawyer who filed a suit for Mr. Roucker against the car dealer.

To file the lawsuit, the lawyer wrote down on a form what had happened to Mr. Roucker. On this form he also wrote that the car dealer should give Mr. Roucker his money back, plus any money Mr. Roucker had spent repairing the car.

The lawyer demanded money for the time Mr. Roucker had spent trying to set the matter straight. An extra sum of money was also requested because Mr. Roucker felt he had been insulted by the car dealer and made to look foolish. The total amount of money Mr. Roucker wanted from the car dealer was $400,000.

Mr. Roucker's lawyer prepared and filed a **complaint.** It gave Mr. Roucker's statement of what happened and asked for compensation. The lawyer filed a request that the court clerk send the car dealer a summons informing her of the lawsuit.

In many states, a summons for a lawsuit is hand delivered by a deputy sheriff or a person hired by the court to serve summons. In others, the summons is sent by mail. When the car dealer received the summons, she had her lawyer prepare an **answer** to the complaint.

The suit was put on the **court docket.** After several months, Mr. Roucker's case came up in court, and a jury was picked to hear it. Remember, the Seventh Amendment in the Bill of Rights guarantees the right to a jury trial in civil cases involving more than $20.00. In this case, either the car dealer or Mr. Roucker could ask for a trial by jury. The case could have been decided by a judge rather than a jury if the car dealer and Mr. Roucker agreed to a trial heard by a judge.

Words to Remember	
answer	legal response to a lawsuit complaint In the *answer,* the car dealer's lawyer explained her side of the case.
complaint	facts of the case and request for damages prepared by the lawyer of the person filing a suit Mr. Roucker's *complaint* asked for $400,000 in compensation.
court docket	a list of cases and the dates when they will be heard in court Mr. Roucker's civil suit was placed on the *court docket* for November 3.

The case took two weeks to hear. During that time, Mr. Roucker's lawyer explained to the jury what had happened. He also presented a written **deposition** from General Motors to the court. This deposition showed that Mr. Roucker's Cadillac had already had 98,000 miles on it a year before he bought it. The mechanic was called to testify. He told the jury what he had found when Mr. Roucker brought his car in for repair. The car dealer's lawyer questioned all of Mr. Roucker's witnesses on the stand. He tried to get them to change their minds about their stories.

The car dealer also got on the witness stand. She said that she did not turn the odometer back. In her opinion, someone had sneaked in during the night and turned it back without anyone knowing it.

After hearing all the testimony and evidence, the jury went into a room and talked about the case. Everyone thought that Mr. Roucker had been cheated. The jury did not believe that the car dealer was telling the truth. In less than an hour, the jury voted 12–0 in favor of Mr. Roucker. The jury came back into the courtroom and told the judge they agreed with the **plaintiff**, Mr. Roucker. The jury also decided that Mr. Roucker should get the $400,000 from the car dealer.

The car dealer did not agree with the decision. She **appealed** the case in an appeals court. She said that there had been many errors in the trying of the case and that the judgment, or sum or money that the jurors had awarded, was too high.

Words to Remember	
appeal	a legal procedure in which a case is presented again for rehearing The car dealer did not agree with the original verdict and *appealed* her case to the appeals court.
deposition	a sworn, written statement that can be used in court The lawyer traveled to New York to take a *deposition* from a witness in the case.
plaintiff	the party that starts a suit against another party, the complainant Mr. Roucker was the *plaintiff* in the suit against the car dealer.

The appeals court did not agree with the car dealer, and she had to pay Mr. Roucker the $400,000.

Small Claims Court

Small claims court is an important way to settle arguments that involve a small sum of money. Suppose someone bought a chair for $250. The chair was to be delivered by the store to the person's apartment. It has been six weeks since the purchase was made, and the store has not delivered the chair. The customer asks the store owner to return the money paid. The store owner refuses and says the customer will get the chair when it is in stock. The customer sues the store owner in small claims court. The store owner is summoned to court.

A lawyer is not needed in small claims court. Of course, a person may have a lawyer for small claims court if he or she wishes to have one. A judge listens to what each person has to say before making a decision. Both sides speak directly to the judge. Witnesses can testify for either side. If the judge agrees that the store owner owes the customer $250, or the chair, then the store owner has to follow the decision. If the judge does not agree that the customer has been cheated, the case is closed.

There are different limits on the amount of money one can sue for in small claims court. In Maryland, for example, the limit is $20,000. The clerk of the small claims court knows the limit in his or her state. The clerk also helps people file the suit papers.

Juvenile Court

A **juvenile** is a person who is not yet an adult. Most states consider anyone who is under the age of 18 to be a juvenile. In some states, the upper age limit for a juvenile is 16 or 17. In most states, a juvenile may not be convicted of any crime except murder. A young person accused and found guilty of a crime is called a **juvenile delinquent**. He or she may be punished but gets special treatment.

	Words to Remember
juvenile	usually a person more than 12 years old and not yet 18 years old, depending on state law He was still a *juvenile* when he was caught stealing hubcaps.
juvenile delinquent	a youth found guilty of committing a crime The *juvenile delinquent* is guilty of shoplifting.

The **juvenile court** is a special court that handles cases involving youth who commit crimes or whose legal guardians find difficult to control. One of the goals of the juvenile court is to help a young person avoid a criminal record. A criminal record will follow the youth for the rest of his or her life.

A **violation** of a law by a young person is called *juvenile delinquency.* The violation may involve committing a crime, either a misdemeanor or a felony. The violation may be against rules that apply only to young people because of their age. These might include **truancy** or curfew violations. Incorrigibility (being out of control) and marrying without permission of a legal guardian are also examples of juvenile offenses.

A juvenile has almost the same rights as an adult. He or she has the right to a lawyer, the right to remain silent, and the right to question witnesses. One right he or she does *not* have is the right to a jury trial. The judge decides what punishment is given a guilty juvenile. Here are some possible punishments:

- The judge might dismiss any charge and just tell the juvenile to behave himself or herself.

- The judge might place the juvenile under the supervision of an agency like the social services department of the probation office.

- The judge might put the juvenile delinquent in a foster home.

- Some juveniles are placed in reformatories or training schools. They must follow certain rules to learn to live in society.

- The judge may have the juvenile returned to his or her parents' care with a warning that stronger action will be taken if he or she misbehaves again.

- A juvenile may be ordered to attend school regularly, do community service jobs for a certain number of hours each week, be at home and in bed by a certain hour, and stay away from certain places and people.

Words to Remember	
juvenile court	a court in which cases against juveniles are heard The procedure is considered a "hearing" rather than a trial because a hearing is more informal than a trial. The goal of the "hearing" is not to put the juvenile in jail, but to get the juvenile to change his or her ways. The case was heard privately in *juvenile court.*
truancy	missing school without permission That student has a long *truancy* record.
violation	the breaking of a law or rule Leaving the school grounds during lunch time is a *violation* of school rules.

In the case of a serious crime, like murder, the state may ask that the juvenile be tried as an adult. The juvenile is then treated like any other accused person. If convicted, he or she can receive a long sentence in jail. A juvenile could even get the death penalty.

Wayward Minor

Some people think that offenders who have passed their sixteenth birthday but are not yet 21 years old should not be treated as criminals, but instead, as "wayward minors." A wayward minor is a person who uses drugs, runs around with the wrong crowd, will not obey his or her parents, or runs away from home. This person has not committed any serious crime, but he or she is behaving so badly that people believe he or she might be committing crimes.

Such a person may be labeled a wayward minor after a court hearing. This person might be placed on **probation.** He or she could also be turned over to a juvenile home for up to three years.

A "youthful offender" is almost the same as a wayward minor, but there is an important difference. A youthful offender has not been convicted of a felony (the most serious type of crime), but he or she *has* been charged with one. For example, James is 17 years old and has been charged with setting fire to a house. He can ask the court to treat him as a youthful offender. If the court agrees, the charge is changed from arson to youthful offense. A "youthful offense" is not a crime, so James will not have a criminal record.

	Word to Remember
probation	a certain period of time during which an offender is watched carefully by someone appointed by the court
	Paul Michael was sentenced to two years' *probation* by the judge.

The scales of justice are balanced to protect and help juveniles.

Minors and the Law

Study the chart below. It shows the steps taken when a young person is arrested. Remember, the juvenile court system in each state will vary. This chart is an example of a typical system.

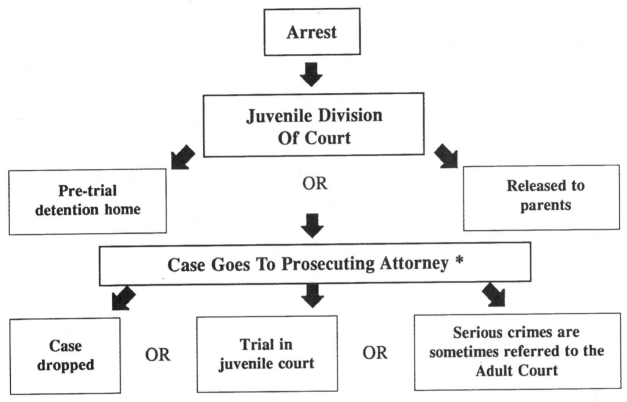

JUVENILE CRIMINAL COURT PROCESS

Arrest

Juvenile Division Of Court

OR

Pre-trial detention home

Released to parents

Case Goes To Prosecuting Attorney *

Case dropped OR **Trial in juvenile court** OR **Serious crimes are sometimes referred to the Adult Court**

* During this time, the young person is either held in pre-trial detention (juvenile institution) or goes home in the custody of his or her parents.

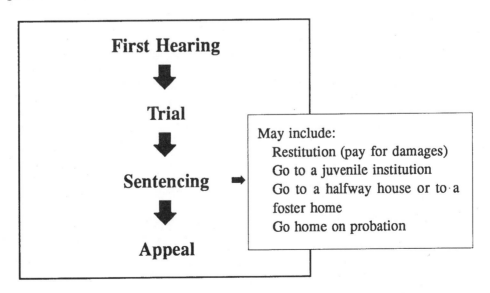

First Hearing

Trial

Sentencing →

Appeal

May include:
Restitution (pay for damages)
Go to a juvenile institution
Go to a halfway house or to a foster home
Go home on probation

Review Unit 6

A Write the letter of the best answer on the line.

_____ 1. What is the court docket?
    a. a person who says, "order in the court"
    b. a list of cases and when they will be heard in court
    c. a sentence of up to one year in jail

_____ 2. A person who loses a civil suit has a right to ____.
    a. complain
    b. appeal to a higher court
    c. appeal to a lower court

_____ 3. A suit for a small amount of money can be held in ____.
    a. the Supreme Court
    b. police court
    c. small claims court

_____ 4. A person who files a lawsuit is called ____.
    a. a plaintiff
    b. a judge
    c. a defendant

_____ 5. In most states, a juvenile may not be convicted of any crime except ____.
    a. car theft
    b. arson
    c. murder

B Match the word to its definition by writing the correct letter on the line provided.

_____ 1. civil suit   a. schedule of upcoming trials
_____ 2. court docket   b. a written statement used as evidence
_____ 3. deposition   c. most serious type of crime
_____ 4. summoned   d. peaceful way to settle an argument
_____ 5. felony   e. ordered to appear in court
_____ 6. appeal   f. statement of facts of a case and a request for damages
_____ 7. answer   g. request for a rehearing of a case
_____ 8. complaint   h. legal response to a complaint

C Each of the following statements is *false*. Rewrite the statement correctly in the space provided.

1. A warranty is a written, formal accusation of a crime.

_____

_____

2. You must have a lawyer to sue in small claims court.

_____

_____

3. Regardless of the crime, a juvenile will not be sent to jail.

_____

_____

4. The goal of the juvenile court is to put a juvenile in jail.

_____

_____

5. A wayward minor is 12–14 years old.

_____

_____

6. A youthful offender has been convicted of a felony.

_____

_____

7. A criminal record is erased after 20 years.

_____

_____

8. A juvenile has exactly the same rights as an adult.

_____

_____

Juvenile Rights—Juvenile or Adult?

Many people feel that juveniles accused of violent crimes (murder, rape, or armed robbery) should be tried as adults. Under our present system, this is possible. The judge decides whether the suspect will be treated as a juvenile and have a hearing in juvenile court or be tried as an adult and have a regular jury trial. In order to reach a decision, a judge considers the following questions:

1. Will the minor be helped by the juvenile system? Can he or she be helped by the juvenile detention (temporary custody) and rehabilitation (helping) program?

2. How serious was the crime? Is it a first offense, or have there been many others? A serious criminal is not likely to be helped by the juvenile system.

3. Was his or her mental condition tested? Can he or she be rehabilitated before becoming an adult?

4. What is his or her personal background: age, parents, school record, job, references?

D Read the following cases. Decide whether the juveniles should be tried as adults or juveniles. Review the section on juvenile court for possible decisions you can make. Also consider the above questions when making your decision. Remember, too, that as the judge, you have the double responsibility: to do what is best for the juvenile and to protect his or her rights, and to do what is best for society and protect people from criminals. Justify your decisions in the space provided.

Case #1

Name: Jan Baker

Age: 16

Charge: Selling controlled dangerous substances (marijuana)

Personal background: High IQ; poor school grades; parents divorced; mother works as a waitress; mother member of Alcoholics Anonymous

Previous record: One conviction for possession of marijuana; served six months on probation

Decision:

_____

_____

Justification:

_____

_____

_____

_____

_____

Case #2

Name: Aaron Petersen

Age: 17 1/2

Charge: Grand theft auto

Personal background: Average student; father deceased; mother works as a
        word processor; no steady job; works at odd jobs in neighborhood

Previous record: No prior arrests

Decision:

_____

_____

Justification:

_____

_____

_____

_____

Case #3

Name: Charles Johnson

Age: 17

Charge: Rape and armed robbery

Personal background: Frequent absences from school; father's address
        unknown; mother works as nurse; psychiatric report shows
        severe emotional problems

Previous record: Convicted of petty theft, burglary

Decision:

_____

_____

Justification:

_____

_____

_____

_____

Case #4

Name: Jonathan Chu

Age: 16

Charge: Assaulting a police officer

Personal background: Extremely bright, but does not work up to ability; father is self-employed; mother does not have a job; Jon works after school at a local supermarket

Previous record: Convicted of robbery; served six months in Youth Training School

Decision:

_____

_____

Justification:

_____

_____

_____

_____

Case #5

Name: Anita Ruiz

Age: 14

Charge: Under-aged drinking and public drunkenness

Personal background: Is an average student; both parents are teachers; feels neglected at home; runs away often, but always returns; was arrested with an adult male

Previous record: None

Decision:

_____

_____

Justification:

_____

_____

_____

_____

Review Units 4–6

A Write the letter of the best answer on the line.

_____ 1. What is the most serious type of criminal act?
   a. a misdemeanor
   b. a felony
   c. a violation

_____ 2. Who decides whether or not you are guilty if you do not have a jury trial?
   a. the lawyers
   b. the bailiff
   c. the judge

_____ 3. Can you have a lawyer if you do not commit a felony?
   a. no
   b. yes, if you cannot afford one
   c. yes, if you are willing to pay the legal fee

_____ 4. If you commit a speeding violation, you ____.
   a. will spend up to six months in jail
   b. may have a right to a jury trial
   c. may have to pay a fine

_____ 5. An example of petty theft is ____.
   a. stealing a car out of a parking lot
   b. robbing a bank in broad daylight
   c. shoplifting CDs at a record store

_____ 6. What is an example of a felony punishable by death?
   a. armed robbery
   b. murder
   c. rape

_____ 7. If you drive the getaway car in a bank robbery and your partner kills one of the tellers while you wait outside, you will be found guilty as ____.
   a. a robber
   b. an accomplice
   c. a criminal

_____ 8. If you are accused of a felony, you have the right to trial by ____.
   a. a jury
   b. a juvenile
   c. a lawyer

_____ **9.** A lawyer is required to ____.
   a. defend the judge
   b. defend the laws of this country
   c. defend his or her client

_____ **10.** What word best describes the lawyer-client relationship?
   a. exclusive
   b. confidential
   c. adversarial

_____ **11.** A lawyer who requires some portion of his or her fee before he or she will take a case is ____.
   a. being unreasonable
   b. requiring a warrant
   c. requiring a retainer

_____ **12.** Judges are ____.
   a. elected
   b. appointed
   c. both of the above

_____ **13.** The jury system requires that ____ be presented to an impartial jury.
   a. defendants
   b. evidence
   c. convictions

_____ **14.** The guilt or innocence of the accused is determined by ____.
   a. the jury
   b. the plaintiff
   c. the lawyers

_____ **15.** Civil rights are those rights that apply to the ____.
   a. government
   b. state
   c. individual

_____ **16.** A person can find out when his or her case will be heard by looking at ____.
   a. the local law bulletin
   b. the court docket
   c. the newspaper

_____ **17.** If you do not agree with the decision of the jury, you may
have the right to ____.

    a. an appeal

    b. a mistrial

    c. a new lawyer

_____ **18.** Small claims court settles disputes involving ____.

    a. petty theft

    b. small sums of money

    c. minor traffic violations

_____ **19.** An important goal of juvenile court is ____.

    a. to lessen the heavy load of cases heard by the regular courts

    b. to crack down on young criminals

    c. to help a young person avoid having a criminal record

_____ **20.** Youthful offenders are minors who have been charged with ____.

    a. misdemeanors

    b. truancy

    c. felonies

B Write the answers to the questions.

1. Can an accomplice be convicted of the same crime as the person who actually committed the crime? Explain.

_____

_____

_____

2. What is the lawyer-client privilege? Does it always apply?

_____

_____

_____

3. Give a brief description of the jury selection process.

_____

_____

_____

You, Drugs, and the Law

People of good sense, I have observed,
seldom fall into disputation.
–Ben Franklin

Words to Remember	
illegal	something that is against the law It is *illegal* to rob a bank.
possess	have on you, or own something Joshua wanted to *possess* a new car.
proscribe	to condemn as harmful or unlawful All the states *proscribe* the use of certain drugs.

The word *drug* means, in its simplest form, "something besides food that is taken into the body and changes the way the body acts." Medicine is considered to be a legal drug. These drugs help sick people get well and are prescribed by a doctor. They are dispensed through licensed pharmacies.

Alcohol is a legal drug for people only after a certain age. The "legal age" varies from state to state. In most states, a person must be at least 21 years old to legally use alcohol. Alcohol affects how fast the body reacts in situations. Driving "under the influence" is a serious problem. About 40 percent of traffic deaths involve drivers who are under the influence of alcohol. Alcohol is a depressant. It slows the reactions of drivers. Drivers under the influence of alcohol become less alert and cannot think as quickly. Their vision may become blurred, and they do not use good judgment. They are a hazard to themselves and to other users of the roadways. Police officers nationwide are on the lookout constantly for drunk drivers. States are passing strong drunk-driving laws.

All states have laws that allow the police to give tests to drivers they believe are drunk. The police officer has to follow a certain procedure before giving these tests. If an officer stops a driver and suspects the driver of being under the influence of alcohol, the officer may ask the driver to perform simple coordination tests. If the officer still suspects the driver is under the influence, he or she may ask the driver to submit to a "breathalyzer test" or a chemical test. If the driver has a certain amount of alcohol in his or her bloodstream, he or she can be charged with driving under the influence of alcohol. Many states consider a blood-alcohol level of .10 as being legally under the influence. On page 69 is an example of what a police officer must say to someone he or she suspects is driving under the influence of alcohol.

Illegal drugs such as cocaine, heroin, and marijuana are **proscribed,** or forbidden, because of the potential harm to the body. It is against the law for anyone to **possess** these drugs.

The body can become addicted to drugs. An addict is someone whose body becomes dependent on a drug to function. This person may become obsessed with getting the drug in any way possible. Drugs are expensive to buy.

An addict may be addicted to illegal drugs such as cocaine, but people can become addicted to legal drugs, too. People can become addicted to medicines. For example, codeine is used in some prescription medicines, such as cough syrups. It is legal to have drugs with codeine in them when they are prescribed by a doctor. However, people can become addicted to codeine.

A person addicted to prescription drugs might go from doctor to doctor, getting prescriptions for the drug. He or she might buy the drugs illegally on the streets. It is illegal to buy prescription drugs without a prescription. People addicted to legal or illegal drugs might be willing to do anything to get the drugs they need. They might steal or even murder to get money to buy the drugs.

Every state in the United States has laws against possessing illegal drugs. In 1988, the United States government passed tougher drug laws. Jail sentences for selling drugs were made longer.

The state has to prove that the substance found on the person is definitely a drug to convict a person of possession of drugs. The state also has to prove that the suspect knew he or she possessed the drug. A person cannot be found guilty of possession if he or she honestly did not know the substance in question was a drug.

Suppose Frank gave a package to his friend, Juanita. Frank did not tell Juanita what was in the package. Juanita put the package in the glove compartment of her car. She was later stopped by a police officer, and the package was found. It contained cocaine. The court would have to be **convinced** that Juanita did not know what was in the package for her to go free. That is not as easy as it sounds. Juanita could have avoided the problem by checking the contents of the package before accepting it.

Possession of an illegal drug is a serious charge. However, a far more serious charge is "possession with **intent** to sell." It is considered a felony to sell drugs.

Words to Remember	
convince	make someone believe something
	He had to *convince* the jury he didn't own the gun.
intent	expect or want to do something
	It was his *intent* to fly around the world.

Usually a court will determine if a person is guilty of possession with intent to sell by considering the amount of drugs found with the person. If a person has a very tiny amount of marijuana on him or her, it is assumed to be too small an amount to sell. It is common sense to believe that someone caught with a suitcase full of cocaine intends to sell the drug to someone else.

In many states, possession of drugs above a certain amount is automatically considered possession with intent to sell. This crime can be punished with many years in jail. In some states, a person could receive 40 years in jail for possession with intent to sell. In some **foreign** countries, mere possession can bring a life sentence.

Many groups in this country are subject to **random** drug testing. The professional baseball, basketball, and football leagues use random drug testing. Any players found to have evidence of drugs in their bodies can be fined, suspended, or even **barred** from the sport. Athletes have ended their careers forever by taking drugs.

In 1988, the United States government passed a rule to **introduce** random drug testing for transportation workers. That means that four million workers—bus drivers, truck drivers, workers in the airline industry, and others—can be tested at any time for drugs. The government decided to start random testing of these workers after a train crash near Baltimore, Maryland, killed 17 people. Two members of the train crew admitted they had been smoking marijuana while they were running the train. One of them went to jail for five years.

Words to Remember	
barred	kept out He was *barred* from playing baseball for one year.
foreign	outside of one's own country Japan is a *foreign* country.
introduce	bring into play, to start something Jeannette had to *introduce* the speaker at the dinner.
random	without definite plan She picked a book at *random* from the shelf.

Chemical Testing for Drunk Drivers

ADVICE OF RIGHTS TO A CHEMICAL TEST
(As provided in Article 10 of the Maryland Vehicle Law)

Any person who drives or attempts to drive a motor vehicle on a highway or on any private property that is used by the public in general in this State is deemed to have consented, with certain limitations, to take a Chemical Test to determine the alcohol content of his blood.

Pursuant to law, I am hereby advising you that you have been stopped or detained and I have reasonable grounds to believe that you have been driving or attempting to drive a motor vehicle while intoxicated or while under the influence of alcohol, or in violation of an Alcohol Restriction. I am further advising you that Maryland Law requires the type of test to be administered shall be the chemical test of breath except that the chemical test of blood shall be the type of test administered if: (1) The defendant is unconscious or otherwise incapable of refusing to take a chemical test for alcohol; (2) Injuries to the defendant require removal of the defendant to a medical facility; or (3) The equipment for administering the chemical test of breath is not available.

The results of such test may be admissible and may be considered with other competent evidence in determining your guilt or innocence in any prosecution relating to your driving or attempting to drive a motor vehicle while intoxicated, while under the influence of alcohol, or in violation of an Alcohol Restriction.

That you have the right to refuse to submit to the test and on your refusal, no test shall be administered.

That if you refuse to submit to the test, it is admissible in evidence in any prosecution relating to your driving or attempting to drive a motor vehicle while intoxicated, while under the influence, or in violation of the Alcohol Restriction.

That your refusal to submit to a chemical test shall result in a suspension of your driver's license and/or driving privilege for not less than 60 days nor more than 6 months for a first offense and not less than 120 days nor more than 1 year for a second or subsequent offense.

That after submitting to a chemical test administered at the request of the arresting officer, you may also have a physician of your choice to administer a chemical test in addition to the one administered at the direction of the police officer.

I have read or have been read the Advice of Rights for Chemical Test and have been advised of administrative penalties that shall be imposed for refusal to take test. I understand that this requested test is in addition to any preliminary road-side test that was taken.

Having been so advised, do you now agree to submit to a Chemical Test to determine the alcohol content of your blood? *(This is not an admission of guilt.)*

(Officer Check Reply)
☐ **YES - Agree to submit to a Chemical Test**   ☐ **NO - Test Refused (Officer Complete Form AB-10C and File).**

Motor Vehicle Driver's Signature _____ Date _____ Time _____

Signature of Officer _____ I.D. No. _____ Police Agency _____

YZ-55(5-55)
As Ordered AB-10C

Mandatory Drug Testing—A Reasonable Request?

The following is an original article that appeared in *The Evening Sun* on Thursday, September 15, 1988 about the National Football League drug plan. After reading the article, answer the five discussion questions on page 74.

The NFL Drug Plan
Will It Stop Drug Abuse in Football?
Substance of NFL Drug Plan Is Still Open to Question

When the first big wave of drug abuse splashed over National Football League shores in May 1977, Bobby Beathard was having dinner with Don Shula at a Miami restaurant.

Two Miami Dolphins, Don Reese and Randy Crowder, had been arrested and charged with dealing cocaine.

Somewhere between the salad and the check, ruining what had been a perfectly good meal, the bad news was delivered by an employee of the Miami Lakes Inn.

"The guy recognized Don and came over to tell us," said Beathard, who was director of player personnel for the Dolphins at the time. "That's when we first found out, sitting at the table.

"We knew a lot less about drugs then we do now. I remember my reaction was one of shock. Now these things don't shock you. It's a shame."

A decade later, drug stories are commonplace in the NFL. The league is awash in substance abuse suspensions, and its 1,400 players are doused with suspicion.

Tuesday's disciplinary action against Leonard Mitchell of Atlanta and Antonio Gibson of New Orleans raised the body count to 19 players who have been suspended for drug or alcohol abuse this season. One of the 19, Chicago's Richard Dent, has appealed his case and awaits a hearing with commissioner Pete Rozelle.

That represents barely more than 1 percent of the league's rank and file. Yet the number is certain to increase under the drug policy drawn up by Rozelle in 1986 and implemented in the summer of 1987.

Under the previous collective bargaining agreement, players were subject to urine testing at each training camp. Under the new policy, Rozelle has empowered the league's drug adviser, Dr. Forest Tennant, Jr., to order random testing of suspected players for reasonable cause.

A first positive test can result in outpatient or inpatient treatment. A second offense draws a 30-day suspension. And a third offense can bring a permanent ban from the league, although the player is entitled to seek reinstatement after one year.

Before this season, only ten NFL players had been disciplined for substance abuse. In just two months, the league has suspended almost twice that many. Included in this year's group are three of the league's top pass rushers—Lawrence Taylor, Dexter Manley, and Bruce Smith—and last year's rushing leader, Charles White. Unknown is the number of first-time offenders.

Does this suggest the program is effective in dealing with the problem?

"I don't know," said Bobby Beathard, who left Miami in 1978 to become general manager of the Washington Redskins. "It's too early to tell. I do know I think it's a positive step, what's happened so far. We have to get these guys out. If they don't learn from the suspensions, I don't know what the answer is.

"I know people say that we have to be supportive and give guys help, and we have been. But there's also another side of it. We don't want these guys in the league."

Unsaid but clearly implied is the NFL's greatest fear; the fear of a scandal so big it would forever taint the league's integrity. That would be a game-throwing scandal.

Image is not the NFL's only incentive to attack the drug problem, though. There is genuine concern for the health of the players. That concern crystallized in June 1986, when Cleveland safety Don Rogers died of a cocaine overdose.

Rogers's death and the New England Patriots' post-Super Bowl drug revelations the same year prodded Rozelle to action. He strongly urged the NFL Management Council and the NFLPA to agree on a strengthened drug program.

When no agreement could be reached, Rozelle laid down the law. In July 1986, he unveiled a new program with plans to impose unilateral random testing. The NFLPA challenged those plans, though, and an arbitrator rejected the random testing.

The schism between management and union only deepened during the strike of 1987. The battle lines now are drawn at players' rights.

"We're still not coping with the problem," Baltimore attorney Tony Agnone said. "Because players and management can't agree on anything, it's become a bargaining chip. We're dealing with men's lives here; we can't be bargaining this issue."

Agnone doesn't think the 30-day suspension is much of a solution, either. "That's only just scratching the surface," he said. "Giving Dexter Manley 30 days off in training camp did nothing but make him out of condition when he came back. Do I think it did anything to curb Dexter? I hope . . . but I'm not a doctor."

Joe Brown, the NFL's director of communications, said the 30-day suspension was in part a message to the players, not a cure.

"What we're trying to do is head off a problem," Browne said. "That's the purpose of the 30 days. We realize 30 days will never be a cure for this. Thirty days is not even halfway there, only part of the way there.

"Still, it's a message to the players that they better straighten out, especially to the occasional users, so they won't be permanently banned."

Rozelle made one significant change in his drug policy this year. That was to place reasonable cause testing in the hands of Tennant. In 1987, it was at the discretion of the clubs. This move, Browne said, took away the conflict of interest when a team might have wanted to keep active a player who had a positive drug test.

The NFLPA begs to differ, of course. In a power struggle it is losing, the union wants a neutral expert to administer reasonable cause testing. Because Tennant, who does not grant interviews, was appointed by Rozelle, the union does not see him as impartial.

"I think he is breaching the doctor-patient relationship that he's supposed to have with the players," said Dick Berthelsen, legal counsel for the NFLPA.

"If he is supposed to address the problem and treat the player, what business has he got in taking what he's learned and sending it to Rozelle and using it as a basis to punish the player?"

Berthelsen said "there's an air of intimidation" in the league now.

"The commissioner has disciplinary powers, we can't deny that," Berthelsen said.

–Reprinted from *The Evening Sun*, Thursday, September 15, 1988

Review Unit 7

A Write the letter of the best answer on the line.

_____ 1. What is a person called who uses drugs a lot?
   a. an addict
   b. a casual offender
   c. a delinquent

_____ 2. What should you do when a friend gives you a package to deliver?
   a. look to see what is in it
   b. throw it away
   c. put it in your pocket

_____ 3. Every state in the United States has laws against ____ drugs.
   a. possessing
   b. drinking
   c. looking at

_____ 4. Possession with intent to sell drugs is always considered a ____.
   a. violation
   b. felony
   c. misdemeanor

_____ 5. Random drug testing can be administered to ____.
   a. professional athletes
   b. airplane pilots
   c. bus drivers
   d. all of the above

B Match the word to its definition by writing the correct letter on the line provided.

_____ 1. drug
_____ 2. random
_____ 3. possess
_____ 4. intent
_____ 5. proscribe

a. to have or to hold
b. with no pattern
c. to make unlawful; to forbid
d. substance taken into your body that changes the way it acts
e. planned action

C Each of the following statements is *false*. Rewrite the statement correctly in the space provided.

1. Drugs like cocaine and heroin are safe if taken in small amounts.

_____

_____

2. You can easily convince a judge that you did not know you were possessing drugs.

_____

_____

3. Possession of an illegal drug is a felony.

_____

_____

4. Possession of a drug results in an automatic life sentence in the United States.

_____

_____

5. Random drug testing is legal in any profession.

_____

_____

6. Alcohol is an illegal drug for all Americans.

_____

_____

7. Heroin is one kind of prescription drug.

_____

_____

8. Only 10 percent of traffic deaths involve drivers under the influence of alcohol.

_____

_____

REVIEW

D Answer the following questions in the space provided. Use these questions for class discussion.

1. Do you think the NFL drug plan will eventually stop its players from using drugs? Why or why not?

_____

_____

_____

_____

2. Why was the Don Reese and Randy Crowder incident such a big cause for concern in 1977?

_____

_____

_____

3. Why do you think an NFL player would continue to use drugs when he knows that he will be suspended from the team if he is caught?

_____

_____

_____

_____

4. Why do you think the NFL implemented this plan? Was it for punishment?

_____

_____

_____

5. Do you think drug testing violates a person's rights? Why or why not? Do you think the drug abuser violates the rights of other people he knows? Why or why not?

_____

_____

_____

_____

Stop and Search

*Conscience is the inner voice which warns us
that someone may be looking.*
–H.L. Mencken

Words to Remember	
neighborhood	an area nearby She lived in the *neighborhood.*
seizure	taking something by force The drugs were subject to *seizure.*
unreasonable	something that is not logical and fair The demand that he fly to the moon was *unreasonable.*
violate	to do harm to something or somebody Did the police officer *violate* the person's rights when she stopped him on the street?

When the 13 original states were part of the British Empire, British soldiers would stop people without good reason. They would ask them questions and take things from them. Sometimes they would put people into jail. The early leaders of our country did not like this. They believed that people should be able to walk the streets of their own country without being stopped by soldiers or police officers for no good reason.

The Fourth Amendment to the Constitution protects the people of this country against **unreasonable** search and **seizure.** That does not mean, of course, that someone can never be stopped, questioned, and searched.

Can a police officer legally stop a person on the street and begin to ask him or her questions? The police officer can if he or she has a reasonable suspicion that some criminal activity is going on or is about to take place. Police cannot stop people just to make them angry or to give them a hard time.

The police can stop people if a crime has been committed in a **neighborhood** where they are walking. One of these people may fit the description of the person who committed the crime. The police would have to have a reason to stop that person and ask him or her questions. Does this **violate** any rights of the individual who is stopped? The final determination would be up to a judge.

The police can search any person that they stop to question for weapons. Again, they have to have a reasonable belief that the person possesses a weapon.

The police must get a warrant from a judge before searching someone and his or her house or car. The police must tell the judge why they want the search. They must convince the judge they have enough reason for the search before the judge will give them a warrant. Examples of applications for search and seizure warrants are on pages 23 and 77.

The warrant must carefully explain what the police are looking for. They can look for nothing else. If the warrant permits a search for drugs, that is all the police can look for. For example, if the warrant is for drugs, the police can go through a person's pockets, or through drawers in a house, looking for drugs. If the search warrant is for a large television, then the police cannot go through pockets or the drawers because the television set could not fit in either place.

There are exceptions to the warrant rule. The police can search a house if the person agrees to it. The police still have limitations. They can do only what was agreed to. If the person agreed to let them search his or her pockets only, they cannot look in the glove compartment of his or her car. The police have to stop their search if requested unless they have found incriminating evidence. Then it is too late.

Amendment 4

The right of the people to be secure in their persons, houses, papers, and effects against unreasonable searches and seizures shall not be violated, and no warrants shall issue, but upon probable cause, supported by oath or affirmation, and particularly describing the place to be searched and the persons or things to be seized.

TO: The Honorable _____, Judge of

the _____ Court, Baltimore County, State of

Maryland

Application is herewith made for a Search and Seizure Warrant in that there is probable cause to believe the laws relating to the illegal manufacturing, distribution, and possession of Controlled Dangerous Substances, as defined in Article 27, Sections 286 and 287 of the Annotated Code of Maryland, 1957 Edition, as amended and revised, dealing generally with Controlled Dangerous Substances, including narcotics, hallucinogenic, and dangerous drugs, are being violated in and upon a certain property and residence located at: _____.

_____

Said property and residence is more particularly described as _____

_____

_____

_____

_____

_____

Furthermore, the said residence can be positively identified by your affiant. The name of your affiant is: _____, of the Criminal Investigation Section.

In support of this application and as the basis for probable cause, your affiant deposes and says:

Your affiant, _____, has been a duly authorized member of the Maryland State Police. Your affiant has received specialized training in the investigation and identification of Controlled Dangerous Substances sponsored by the Maryland State Police Narcotics Section and the Federal Drug Enforcement Administration. Additionally, your affiant has assisted in numerous Search and Seizure Warrants pertaining to violations of the Controlled Dangerous Substance laws of the State of Maryland.

A police officer does not need a search warrant if a certain object is in "plain view." Suppose, for instance, a police officer looked in a car and saw a television set that fit the description of a stolen television set. If the police have a reasonable belief that there is evidence of a crime in a car, they do not need a warrant to search it. The reason for this is that someone could easily drive away before the police officers could get a search warrant.

The police cannot choose a car for no reason and search it. If they have searched a car and found something illegal, they still have to convince a judge that they had a good reason to stop the car in the first place.

All of this might sound confusing, and sometimes it is because different people look at things in different ways. The thing to remember is that the police must have a good reason for stopping and searching and will eventually have to convince a judge that they had a good reason.

The situation changes a lot when a person is actually arrested. Suppose a man is seen running from a bank that has just been robbed. The man is caught by the police, and a bag full of money is found on him. The police arrest him. When this person is arrested, he can be searched without giving his permission.

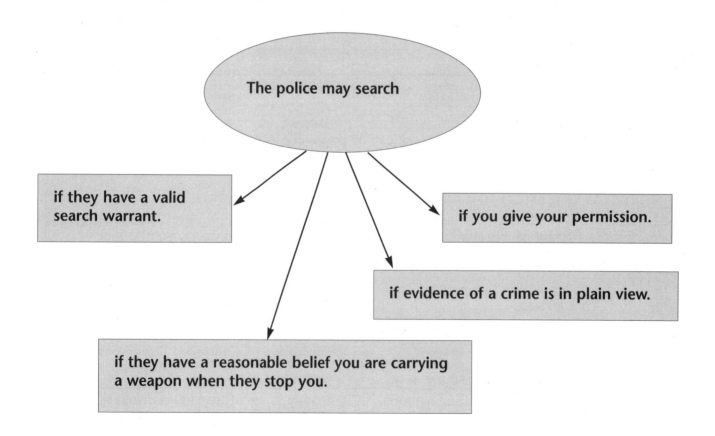

The police may search

if they have a valid search warrant.

if you give your permission.

if evidence of a crime is in plain view.

if they have a reasonable belief you are carrying a weapon when they stop you.

Review Unit 8

A Write the letter of the best answer on the line.

_____ 1. Which amendment to the U.S. Constitution protects a citizen from unreasonable search and seizure?
   a. the First Amendment
   b. the Third Amendment
   c. the Fourth Amendment

_____ 2. When can the police legally stop someone and ask that person questions?
   a. when the police have a reasonable belief that something is wrong
   b. when the police see that person crossing the street against the light
   c. when the police see that person with his or her hands in his or her pockets

_____ 3. Citizens are protected from ____ search and seizure.
   a. unreasonable
   b. quick
   c. reasonable

_____ 4. The police can legally search a person for ____.
   a. buttons
   b. playing cards
   c. weapons

_____ 5. What is the main thing to remember about stopping and searching?
   a. that the police must have a good reason
   b. that you should stay off the streets at all times
   c. that the police have no right to do this

B Find each word in bold type in the text. Think about what the word means in that sentence. Then match the word to its definition by writing the correct letter on the line provided.

_____ 1. seizure   a. consent; authorization

_____ 2. violate   b. to disregard

_____ 3. incriminating c. showing sound judgment

_____ 4. permission   d. proving involvement

_____ 5. reasonable   e. taking possession

_____ 6. unreasonable f. to cause to believe

_____ 7. convince   g. not logical

C Each of the following statements is *false*. Rewrite the statement correctly in the space provided.

1. The police can stop and search you at any time.

_____

_____

2. If the police are searching your house for a stolen television, they can go through all of your kitchen cabinets.

_____

_____

3. The police need a search warrant even if you have given them permission.

_____

_____

4. Citizens are protected from immediate search and seizure.

_____

_____

5. The police must get a warrant from a lawyer before they can search someone.

_____

_____

6. The Fourth Amendment says that a search and seizure warrant does not have to identify the place to be searched or the goods to be seized.

_____

_____

7. The police cannot search you if they have reasonable belief you are carrying a weapon.

_____

_____

8. If the police are searching your home without a warrant and you ask them to stop, they must stop under any circumstances.

_____

_____

Review Units 7–8

■ Circle the letter of the best answer.

_____ 1. Proscribed drugs are ____.
   a. illegal
   b. legal
   c. expensive

_____ 2. Alcohol is a drug that is ____.
   a. legal
   b. illegal
   c. legal, after a certain age

_____ 3. If you are an addict, you are ____.
   a. in possession of drugs
   b. someone who sells drugs
   c. dependent on drugs

_____ 4. Possession of an illegal drug is ____ "possession with intent to sell."
   a. more serious than
   b. less serious than
   c. equally as serious as

_____ 5. The amount of drugs found in your possession indicates ____.
   a. whether or not you are an addict
   b. how often you use drugs
   c. whether or not you are involved in the sale of drugs

_____ 6. Random drug testing was introduced by the U.S. government
   in 1988 for ____.
   a. office workers
   b. athletes
   c. transportation workers

_____ 7. In some foreign countries, the possession of drugs is grounds for ____.
   a. exile
   b. life in prison
   c. the death penalty

_____ 8. According to the Fourth Amendment of the Constitution, under what
   circumstances can the police stop and question someone on the street?
   a. at any time
   b. if the police think that the person may know something
   c. if the police have a reasonable suspicion

_____ 9. Searching an individual for weapons can ____.

    a. never occur without a warrant

    b. occur at any time

    c. occur whenever the police have a reasonable belief that the person possesses a weapon

_____ 10. A warrant to search for a stolen bicycle will not allow the police to look ____.

    a. in dresser drawers

    b. in hall closets

    c. in the basement

_____ 11. An exception to the warrant rule is ____.

    a. the judge's consent

    b. the homeowner's consent

    c. the lawyer's consent

_____ 12. When the police remove the drugs from your possession, ____.

    a. an arrest has taken place

    b. a robbery has taken place

    c. a seizure has taken place

_____ 13. ____ evidence tends to convict someone.

    a. Hard

    b. Incriminating

    c. Convincing

_____ 14. An example of a prescription drug that a person could become addicted to is ____.

    a. codeine

    b. heroin

    c. alcohol

_____ 15. About ____ percent of traffic deaths involve drivers under the influence of alcohol.

    a. 15

    b. 40

    c. 60

_____ 16. In many states you are considered legally under the influence of alcohol if your blood-alcohol level is ____.

    a. .001

    b. .01

    c. .10

End-of-Book Test

T
E
S
T

A The following statements are either true or false. Write *True* on the line next to a statement that is true and *False* on the line next to a statement that is false.

_____ 1. The American system of law has its roots in the Roman and English systems of law.

_____ 2. A person accused of a crime is considered guilty until proven innocent in criminal law.

_____ 3. The thirteen American colonies declared their independence from France in 1776.

_____ 4. A republic is a democracy in which people elect leaders to represent them in government.

_____ 5. The First Article of the Constitution set up the judicial branch of government.

_____ 6. The Congress is the executive, or law-enforcing, branch of government.

_____ 7. Freedom of speech is one of the rights guaranteed in the Bill of Rights.

_____ 8. The Fifth Amendment provides that if a person is found innocent of a crime, he or she cannot be tried for the same crime again.

_____ 9. The Eighth Amendment allows any amount of bail in all cases.

_____ 10. Police must read people they arrest their Miranda rights before questioning them.

_____ 11. A misdemeanor is the most serious type of crime.

_____ 12. A person who has been acquitted of a crime has been found guilty.

_____ 13. A lawsuit is a civil law case.

_____ 14. A 14-year-old who is found guilty of a crime is called a *juvenile delinquent.*

_____ 15. All cases in juvenile courts are heard in public.

_____ 16. Codeine is an example of a prescription drug.

_____ 17. Transportation workers must submit to random drug testing.

_____ 18. Police can search your home without a warrant if they have your neighbor's permission.

_____ 19. "Pleading the Fifth" means that you refuse to answer questions that might incriminate you.

_____ 20. Possession of marijuana is not a crime.

B Write the letter of the best answer on the line.

_____ 1. Roman law protected ____.
   a. the state from the individual
   b. the guilty from prosecution
   c. the individual from the state

_____ 2. The lower house of the Congress is called the ____.
   a. Parliament
   b. House of Representatives
   c. Senate

_____ 3. The President of the United States can ____.
   a. pass bills
   b. veto bills
   c. override vetoes

_____ 4. The civil rights marches led by Dr. Martin Luther King, Jr., were examples of exercising the freedom of ____.
   a. assembly
   b. the press
   c. religion

_____ 5. The grand jury can ____ a person for a crime.
   a. arrest
   b. indict
   c. try

_____ 6. Someone who steals a truck would be charged with ____.
   a. grand theft
   b. petty theft
   c. a violation

_____ 7. A lawyer who works for a publishing company is a ____ lawyer.
   a. family
   b. criminal
   c. corporate

_____ 8. In a criminal trial, a jury that cannot reach a verdict is known as a ____.
   a. impartial jury
   b. grand jury
   c. hung jury

C Use the terms in the box to complete the following sentences. Write the terms on the lines.

Word Box

Bill of Rights	conflict	Constitution
court docket	deposition	intent
judicial	Miranda	monetary
nullified	petition	probation
prosecutor	searches	summons

---

1. A _____ is a list of cases and the dates they will be heard in court.

2. The citizen received a _____ to appear in the jury pool room on Monday.

3. Because the judge sentenced the juvenile to _____, the juvenile will have to report to a court-appointed authority.

4. The defendant was arrested for the possession of drugs with the _____ to sell.

5. If a police officer does not follow procedures during an arrest, the charges against

   the accused could be _____.

6. The _____ of the United States has seven articles and 27 amendments.

7. The Supreme Court is part of the _____ branch of government.

8. The first ten amendments of the Constitution are known as the _____.

9. The First Amendment guarantees freedom to _____ the government.

10. The Fourth Amendment protects individuals from unreasonable _____.

11. The right to have a lawyer present when being questioned by the police is one

    of the _____ rights.

12. The _____ value involved in a crime may be used to determine if the crime is a misdemeanor or a felony.

13. In criminal court, the _____ is the lawyer who represents the state.

14. A _____ is a sworn, written statement that can be used in court.

15. State constitutions cannot include laws that _____ with the Constitution of the United States.

**T
E
S
T**

D Answer the following questions in complete sentences.

1. Why did the Constitutional Convention write the Constitution?

_____

_____

_____

2. How are juvenile court proceedings like adult criminal court proceedings? How do they differ?

_____

_____

_____

3. Describe two ways in which police can search your home and still be following procedures.

_____

_____

_____

4. What are the purpose and duties of a jury in a criminal trial?

_____

_____

_____

5. Describe a situation in which a person could be convicted for being an accomplice in a crime.

_____

_____

_____

6. Are there any circumstances in which you think juveniles accused of serious crimes should be tried as adults? Explain your answer.

_____

_____

_____

Facts to Remember

Here are some interesting facts about the law.

> ➤ In most states, a man and woman must have the permission of their parents to marry if the man and woman are under the age of 18. They do not need the permission from their parents if they can prove they are self-supporting, even if they are under 18 years of age.

> ➤ A person stopped for a speeding violation is required to give his or her name and address and the names and addresses of passengers in the car. He or she also has to give the officer a registration card and driver's license.

> ➤ If a car is stolen or destroyed, car payments have to be continued.

> ➤ Parents have the right to make their children behave. Parents can persuade their children to do what they want them to do by using reasonable force.

> ➤ All states have laws against drunk driving. A person can be arrested, fined, and jailed if caught driving while under the influence of alcohol. A drunken driver may also lose his or her license to drive. All states have laws that allow the police to give tests to drivers they believe to be drunk. A driver cannot be forced to take these tests. But if he or she refuses, he or she may lose his or her license to drive, even if a judge later rules that the driver was not drunk.

> ➤ A landlord (the person who owns the property) can evict a tenant (the person who rents the place from the landlord) any time the tenant violates his lease (a written agreement) with the landlord. Tenants are usually evicted (thrown out) for not paying the rent, but they can be evicted for making loud noises at night, using the apartment for illegal purposes, or any number of other reasons.

Glossary Activities

The glossary includes words and phrases related to the law. The following glossary activities can help you understand and use the glossary terms. You can check your answers to the activities by looking up the words in the glossary.

Word Search

A Definitions are written below for the words to be found in the puzzle. Write the missing word beside the definition. Then circle the word in the puzzle. (Hint: The definitions are in alphabetical order.)

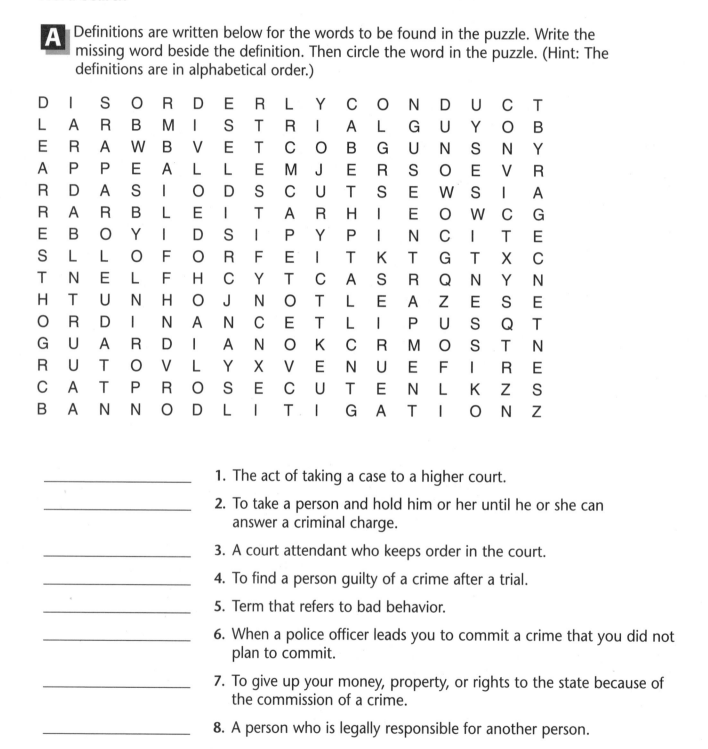

```
D  I  S  O  R  D  E  R  L  Y  C  O  N  D  U  C  T
L  A  R  B  M  I  S  T  R  I  A  L  G  U  Y  O  B
E  R  A  W  B  V  E  T  C  O  B  G  U  N  S  N  Y
A  P  P  E  A  L  L  E  M  J  E  R  S  O  E  V  R
R  D  A  S  I  O  D  S  C  U  T  S  E  W  S  I  A
R  A  R  B  L  E  I  T  A  R  H  I  E  O  W  C  G
E  B  O  Y  I  D  S  I  P  Y  P  I  N  C  I  T  E
S  L  L  O  F  O  R  F  E  I  T  K  T  G  T  X  C
T  N  E  L  F  H  C  Y  T  C  A  S  R  Q  N  Y  N
H  T  U  N  H  O  J  N  O  T  L  E  A  Z  E  S  E
O  R  D  I  N  A  N  C  E  T  L  I  P  U  S  Q  T
G  U  A  R  D  I  A  N  O  K  C  R  M  O  S  T  N
R  U  T  O  V  L  Y  X  V  E  N  U  E  F  I  R  E
C  A  T  P  R  O  S  E  C  U  T  E  N  L  K  Z  S
B  A  N  N  O  D  L  I  T  I  G  A  T  I  O  N  Z
```

_____ 1. The act of taking a case to a higher court.

_____ 2. To take a person and hold him or her until he or she can answer a criminal charge.

_____ 3. A court attendant who keeps order in the court.

_____ 4. To find a person guilty of a crime after a trial.

_____ 5. Term that refers to bad behavior.

_____ 6. When a police officer leads you to commit a crime that you did not plan to commit.

_____ 7. To give up your money, property, or rights to the state because of the commission of a crime.

_____ 8. A person who is legally responsible for another person.

_____ 9. To stir up someone or some group to do something.

_____ 10. A body of men and women selected to try an accused person.

_____ 11. A lawsuit.

_____ 12. A trial that ends without a verdict

_____ 13. A local law

_____ 14. To carry forward a legal proceeding.

_____ 15. A penalty given to a person convicted of a crime.

_____ 16. To give evidence in court under oath.

_____ 17. A place where a crime is committed.

_____ 18. A person who hears, sees, or knows something and testifies in court.

Bonus: Hidden in the word search puzzle are two more legal terms not defined. What are they? Look up their definitions in the glossary. Write each word and its definition here.

1. _____

_____

_____

_____

_____

2. _____

_____

_____

_____

_____

Challenge and Check

B Read the following list of legal terms. Without looking the words up in the glossary, determine if the terms relate to money or to real estate. Place an *M* in front of the word if you think it should go in the *Money* category or *R* if it describes something in *Real Estate*.

_____ 1. lease

_____ 2. embezzlement

_____ 3. lien

_____ 4. ransom

_____ 5. eviction

_____ 6. trespass

_____ 7. retainer

_____ 8. robbery

_____ 9. garnishee

_____ 10. squatter

_____ 11. extortion

_____ 12. contract

_____ 13. assets

_____ 14. bail

_____ 15. deed

_____ 16. domicile

_____ 17. bribery

_____ 18. fiduciary

_____ 19. insolvent

_____ 20. tenant

C Look up the words listed above in the glossary. Read the definitions. Write each word in the correct column: *Money* or *Real Estate*. Then check your work in the activity above to see how good your legalese is.

Money

1. _____
2. _____
3. _____
4. _____
5. _____
6. _____
7. _____
8. _____
9. _____
10. _____
11. _____
12. _____

Real Estate

1. _____
2. _____
3. _____
4. _____
5. _____
6. _____
7. _____
8. _____
9. _____
10. _____

Spell Check

D Legal terms found in the glossary are listed below. However, one letter is missing in each word. You are a detective, and your assignment is to find the missing letter. Write the letter in the space provided. Then rewrite the entire word.

1. ar ____ on   _____

2. p ____ obate   _____

3. consp ____ racy   _____

4. malpracti ____ e   _____

5. t ____ eft   _____

6. inh ____ ritance   _____

7. ac ____ used   _____

8. fr ____ ud   _____

9. l ____ rceny   _____

10. in ____ ictment   _____

Super-Sleuth

E The following words are legal terms found in the glossary. Write the words alphabetically in the space provided. Check the order by looking the words up in the glossary.

1. levy   _____

2. pilfer   _____

3. affidavit   _____

4. inquest   _____

5. rehabilitate _____

6. homicide   _____

7. murder   _____

8. acquit   _____

9. burglary   _____

10. malice   _____

Detective Definitions

F Definitions are written for words in the glossary. Your assignment is to decide what word is being defined. Evidence is given to help you solve the problem.

1. A person who takes part in the commission of a crime.

   a c __ __ __ __ __ __ __ e

2. A defense in which the accused person tries to prove he or she was somewhere else when the crime was committed.

   __ l __ b __

3. Refusing to buy a certain company's products.

   b __ y __ __ __ __

4. A person who starts a suit against someone else.

   c __ __ p __ __ __ n __ __ __

5. Postponement of a hearing or trial.

   c __ __ t __ __ __ __ __ __ __

6. To cheat or trick someone out of money or property.

   d __ __ __ __ __ d

7. Forbidden by law.

   __ l l __ __ __ __

8. A promise to do something.

   o __ __ __

9. A court proceeding in which a plaintiff says he or she has been wronged by another person and wants justice.

   s __ __ t

10. The final decision by a judge or jury as to guilt or innocence.

    __ __ r __ __ __ t

Glossary

A

abet: To aid or encourage someone to commit a crime.

abscond: To hide or leave town to avoid the law.

accessory: A person who is involved in the commission of a crime, whether that person committed the crime or not, or was even there when the crime was committed.

accomplice: A person who takes part in the commission of a crime.

accused: A person charged with committing a crime.

acquit: To find not guilty of a crime.

adversary proceeding: A contest in court between two parties.

affidavit: A written statement of fact sworn to by the person stating the fact or facts.

alibi: A defense in which the accused person tries to prove he or she was somewhere else when a crime was committed.

appeal: The act of taking a case to a higher court after losing that case in a lower court.

arbitration: The settlement of an argument between two parties by a third party. In baseball, for example, if the owner of a team and one of the team's players can't agree on how much money a player should be paid, a third party can be brought in to decide the amount.

arraign: A person is called into court to hear the charges against him and is asked to plead guilty or not guilty. This is called an arraignment.

arrest: To take a person and hold him or her until he or she can answer a criminal charge.

arson: Illegally burning something, often a house, on purpose.

assault: Trying to harm, or threatening to harm, someone physically.

assets: All the property and money you own. Your shirt is an asset, as is the money in your pocket.

attorney-at-law: A person who has been trained and licensed to practice law. Same as a lawyer.

B

bail: A sum of money given to the court to get the release of an accused person from jail until his or her trial.

bailiff: Court attendant who keeps order in the court and looks after the jury's needs.

battery: Unlawful use of force against one person by another. If you start a fight and hit someone in the jaw with your fist, you can be accused of battery.

boycott: To refuse to buy a certain company's products.

bribery: Giving someone money to get him or her to do something illegal. The driver tried to bribe the police officer by offering the officer $20 to forget the speeding ticket.

burglary: Breaking into a building with the intent to steal something.

C

change of venue: Moving a trial from one place to another.

commutation: Reduction of a sentence.

complainant: A person who starts a suit against someone else.

conspiracy: An agreement between two or more parties to commit an illegal act.

contempt of court: Refusal to do as a court asks. Usually punished by a fine or imprisonment.

continuance: Postponement of a hearing or trial.

contract: An agreement, usually in writing, between two parties to do or not do something. You would sign a contract with a builder to construct your house. The contract would state what features you want in your house. By signing the contract, the builder would agree to build it the way you want. If he or she does not, you can sue him or her.

convict: To find a person guilty of a crime after a trial.

coroner: A public official who investigates a sudden or violent death to see if anything unlawful has occurred.

corroborate: To back up something someone else said. If James said he was at home at the time the bank was robbed and you said you saw him at home at that time, you would be corroborating his statement.

GLOSSARY

D

deed: A written document by which property is transferred from one person to another. If you sold your house, you would have to give the deed to the house to the new owner. This would prove that the new owner had paid you for the house.

defamation: The act of saying bad things about another person.

default: Failure to fulfill a legal obligation. If you haven't paid the mortgage on your house, you have defaulted.

defraud: To cheat or trick someone out of money or property.

delinquent: A person who commits a crime or fails to do something he or she was supposed to do, such as paying his or her bills.

disorderly conduct: This generally refers to bad conduct, like getting drunk and cursing people on the street, and can be punished by a fine or short jail sentence.

domicile: A place where a person lives.

E

embezzlement: This is what happens when someone to whom you have entrusted your money steals it.

eminent domain: The right of a city or state to take your property after paying you a fair price for it.

entrapment: This is what happens when a police officer leads you to commit a crime that you had not planned to commit.

eviction: If someone doesn't pay his or her rent, he or she can be evicted, or forced to leave legally, by the owner of the house or apartment.

evidence: Anything that gives facts at a trial. Fingerprints on a gun can be evidence.

extortion: Getting money from someone by threatening him or her.

extradition: If you committed a crime in Maryland and were caught in West Virginia, Maryland would have to extradite you from the other state. This is a constitutional protection of an accused person. He or she can't just be sent from one state to another without a judge agreeing to it.

F

false pretense: A lie someone tells in order to cheat someone else.

fiduciary: A person who handles someone else's money or property.

fine: A sum of money paid as a penalty for violating a law. A person caught speeding usually has to pay a fine.

foreclosure: If a person doesn't pay the mortgage (monthly payment, usually to a bank, of money that person owes) on his or her house, the bank can foreclose, or take the house away and sell it.

forfeit: To give up your money, property, or rights to the state because of the commission of a crime.

fraud: Any illegal trick that gets money or property from another person.

G

garnish: If you owe money to another party, that party can go to your employer and garnish your wages. That means the employer will have to give part of your wages (the amount is usually determined by a judge) to the party you owe the money to.

guardian: A person or persons legally responsible for another person and his or her property. Your parents are your guardians until you reach a certain age set by law.

H

heir A person who inherits property and money from a person who has died.

homicide: The killing of any person by another person.

I

illicit: Forbidden by law.

incite: To stir up someone or a group to do something. The man incited the mob to break windows.

incriminate: To connect a person with a crime.

indictment: A formal, written charge of crime given by a grand jury. The next step is trial of the accused.

infraction: Violation of the laws.

inheritance: The passing of money and property to an heir or heirs (an *heir* is a person who inherits).

injunction: An order issued by a court to make someone do something or to stop him or her from doing it. A judge might give an order (an injunction) to a union to make the union